God Speaks

Short study guide on Biblical Interpretation using Hebrews

Evan R C Reynolds

Edited by Ruth Aird

Evan Richard Charles Reynolds
1932-1987

Works also by Ruth Aird

History: Revealing Your Genesis

Letters to Jennifer

Seven Letters from Patmos

Our esteemed brother in the Lord, in his characteristically unique and original style, has based his study on the Epistle to the Hebrews, the most appropriate New Testament book to use as a model of sound exposition and relevant application to its first readers' lives. The result is both Christ-exalting and challenging.

Malcom Davies, Author

Overall, my view is that this could be a useful publication for those who may be beginning serious Bible study. The emphasis on the use of the Old Testament is good, given how many Christians seem to avoid it!

Bill Stevely, Bible Teacher

Evan had a unique and unmistakable prayerful style with a deep understanding of the scriptures, which made everyone think it through carefully for themselves. He truly was an encouraging teacher of the Word, bringing out different aspects which were a result of detailed and prayerful study, appreciated by young and old alike.

Hugh Piper, Wallingford Christian Assembly

The Book of Hebrews is a treasure trove which expounds Old Testament Scripture, giving meaning to passages a modern reader might feel a bit obscure. It is indeed, as this Study Guide reminds us, 'God's correspondence course.' Through the pages of Hebrews we time travel through the Old Testament with an expert guide, Evan Reynolds, a scholar who was in love with the Book and in love with the Lord.

Jenny Robertson, Scottish Author

This book will be of much interest and benefit to serious students of God's Word. Evan Reynolds has a systematic and incisive way of methodically interpreting Scripture. I was also deeply touched by the letters, comments and poem at the end of the work.

Eric Scott, Elder, Carrubers Christian Fellowship, Edinburgh

2021 Beithe Publishing

A Short Guide to Interpreting the Word of God: How to read the Bible using the book of Hebrews

Manuscript first handwritten 1987; Deciphered and typed October 2020; Published 2022

Author Evan R C Reynolds

Additional excerpts provided by Mr Malcolm Davis

Edited and additions provided by Ruth Aird

Requests for information or any comments should be directed to ruth@reaird.plus.com

All photographic illustrations belong to Joan Reynolds

Front cover artwork by Elizabeth Rigg: original canvas 'The Rent Curtain' on display in Bruntsfield Evangelical Church, Edinburgh

Graphic Design by Esther Ferrier
estherjaneferrier@gmail.com

All scripture quotations are taken from the New International Version of the Bible 1984 International Bible Society unless otherwise stated.

ff. in the references means 'and the verses following the first given'.

A record of this book is available from the British Library ISBN: 978-1-8381181-2-9

Beithe Publishing 13 Mauricewood Bank Penicuik EH26 0BS

Printed in Great Britain by Bell and Bain Ltd, Glasgow

DEDICATION

To the believers who gather at Wallington (Ross Road ~ 1943-1957)
Farnham (Weydon Lane ~ 1957 – 1959)
Oxford (James Street ~ 1959-1980)
Dehra Dun, India (Old Connaught Place 1986)
Wallingford (Station Fields 1980-1988)

Since baptism I have had the privilege of fellowship with the above five companies. Amongst these believers I began to love the Scriptures, learn to interpret them, and use them to our mutual benefit. The experience gained in bringing the Word of God to these and many other companies, some very small, has been of incalculable value to me. I acknowledge my gratitude for invitations to preach, for encouragement and, I might add, endurance. Beyond all, I testify to the gentle persistence of the greatest teacher, the Holy Spirit - yet any waywardness you notice in the following pages is entirely mine.

Evan R C Reynolds

Evan R C Reynolds

Wallingford, Oxon 1987

A good name is more desirable than great riches.
To be esteemed is better than silver or gold
Proverbs 22:1

Short Bio on ERCR

Evan Richard Charles Reynolds was born in 1932 Wallington, Surrey. He came from a Methodist background, with godly Christian parents who had originally wanted to go out to India as missionaries. However, the first world war interrupted their desire and Ernest Reynolds was interned in Dartmoor prison as a conscientious objector. Meanwhile, Emily Penn, his fiancée, gained her degree in Chemistry at Bedford College, London, after which she worked with the Imperial College Research team on the physiological effects of tobacco. Her short career as a scientist ended with marriage and bringing up two boys, Geoffrey, and Evan. However, she was to pass on her scientific knowledge to both boys who went on to be well known in their own chosen fields of science. While these august beginnings are a story in themselves there is no doubt that they had a profound influence on the young Evan.

The family had by this time moved to the Brethren Assembly in Ross Road, Wallington, but Evan's father often preached in other Assemblies in the Home Counties, notably supporting the new church which they helped to establish with Ernest's brother Harold, in South Bermondsey, London.

During the Second World War, Evan was still at school. He was then awarded a place at Imperial College, London. His doctorate was written at Alice Holt in Hampshire, after which he became a lecturer for the Forestry Commission at Oxford University. By this time, he was married to Joan Symondson and moved to the village of Kennington just outside Oxford where they brought up their three children Ruth, Mark, and Paul.

It was here that Evan started his biblical studies in earnest. Every spare moment was spent either preparing sermons or personal study which he would take to local village assemblies, some meeting in little cottages or out in the open air. No meeting of Christians was too small or rural for him to attend and expound the riches of the Word of God. Very often on a Sunday evening the whole family plus friends would bundle into an ancient, creaking Bedford van and arrive at a little cottage or meeting hall with a roaring fire. There, in the dull light of 1960s electricity, the Bible would be opened, and people's faces would shine in the darkness as they listened to the earnest entreaties of a young man passionately sharing his faith from the living and vibrant Word that he had discovered through his studies.

In his professional capacity as a lecturer at Oxford University he opened his rooms to students once a week, where they would study the Bible together. These students would go onto become ministers, missionaries, camp leaders and lay preachers around the world.

Thirty years later, and just a few hours before he laid down his Bible and pen for the last time, Evan left a legacy for all those who want to study the Word of God as he did. He has passed on the baton to all of you who will read this book and desire to know God with as deep and rich an intent as himself. He utterly understood the Psalmist when he said:

How sweet are your words to my taste, sweeter than honey to my mouth! Ps 119:103

He went into the presence of his Lord on December 23rd, 1987, with his Bible open on his lap, reading the words of Revelation and a smile on his face.

They will see his face, and his name will be on their foreheads. There will be no more night. They will not need the light of a lamp or the light of the sun, for the Lord God will give them light. And they will reign for ever and ever. Rev 22; 4,5

Contents   Page

Forword   Malcolm Davies   15
How to use this book   17
Introduction   21
Chapter One   Equipping God's People   29
Chapter Two   The Epistle to the Hebrews   35
Chapter Three   Debt to other writers   43
Chapter Four   The Power of Interpreted Scripture   55
Chapter Five   Interpretive Methods and Helps   62
Chapter Six   Quoting Scripture   74
Chapter Seven   Translations   81
Chapter Eight   Word Studies   92
Chapter Nine   Chronology   102
Chapter Ten   The Case for Dispensations   107
Chapter Eleven   Bible Prophecy   118
Chapter Twelve   Bible Topics   123
Chapter Thirteen   Biblical Biography   129
Chapter Fourteen   Hebrew Ritual Interpreted   133
Chapter Fifteen   What is Typology?   138
Chapter Sixteen   An Antidote to Carnal Religion   148
Chapter Seventeen Case Studies: 154
                     A Kadesh Barnea   155
                     B Melchizedek   163
                     C Comparison of Old and New   170
                     Testament quotes from Hebrews
                     D Jehoshaphat and the beauty of Holiness   176
Chapter Eighteen   The Matter before the Method – the
                     student's study assessment   184
Epilogue   192
Acknowledgments   200
References   202

Contents   Page

Appendix 1   Explanation of the significance of Biblical
               numbers   206
Appendix 2   *Types, Patterns and Shadows* Reynolds E
               Davis M   208

Table 1:   Methods of Biblical interpretation used in
               Hebrews   45
Table 2:   Most commonly used Bible Translations   85
Table 3:   Items of worship from the Old Testament
               tabernacle in Hebrews   134
Table 4:   Numerical table of characters in Hebrews   206
Table 5:   Greek/English words used by translators in
               the Authorised Version   209

               Illustrations:
               El Momento, Lima National Art Gallery,
               Lima, Peru   72
               The Tabernacle, Counties Evangelist
               Exhibition by Phil Widdison   141

               Subject Index   214

FOREWORD

This book has been a work in progress ever since 1987, when Evan Reynolds completed the first draft shortly before he was called Home to glory at a tragically early age. His daughter, Ruth Aird, has undertaken the task of revising and preparing it for the press. References postdating 1987 are her editorial work, carried out well in the light of later relevant publications, many very recent. Some other friends of the family have also contributed helpful comments and been involved with the task of proofreading. Ruth asked me to contribute to her editorial work a few years ago, which I have been happy to do. We all trust that the resulting publication will prove to be of benefit to all readers and interpreters of Holy Scripture, which we firmly believe to be God's infallible Word to each one of us, as relevant today as it was when it was first written.

Understanding how to interpret Scripture correctly according to sound principles is vital before we try to apply its truth to our daily lives. There have over the centuries been many different attempts to do so, with varying results, so a concise guide to the task is very welcome. Our esteemed brother in the Lord, in his characteristically unique and original style, has based his study on the Epistle to the Hebrews, the most appropriate New Testament book to use as a model of sound exposition and relevant application to its first readers' lives. The result is both Christ-exalting and challenging.

Evan Reynolds was well-qualified to write this guide to help the Lord's people, since he exemplified true Christian qualities in his daily life and had a very genuine shepherd heart. Many students and older members of the assemblies where he was in fellowship can testify to this; for instance, he helped me during a time of serious illness. His home, ably run by his wife Joan, was a place of warm Christian fellowship and hospitality every week for many years.

The guide will be of especial interest to those who knew our brother, including those he visited in India on a few occasions, when he taught forestry and advised the government there. However, it is hoped that it may have a somewhat wider readership amongst assemblies and other evangelical Christians. I recommend the book to them wholeheartedly, and trust that it will result in the Lord's greater glory.

Malcolm Davis, Leeds, January 2022.

How to use this book

When this book was first written it was with the express purpose of giving the simple means by which anyone who wanted to study the Word of God and know Him who; 'through the blood of the eternal covenant brought back from the dead our Lord Jesus' (Heb 13:20), could do so with a modicum of understanding.

Thirty four years have passed since that first handwritten manuscript and in that period of time the world has gone through unprecedented change which has rendered it almost unrecognisable. The greatest change has been our entrance into a digital age and so one might think that a text such as this one, written in longhand with references from an era with Queen Victoria on the throne, might not have relevance for us today. However, nothing could be further from the truth.

Before a pilot can fly the principles of aerodynamics are required as a prerequisite of learning. Before a nurse can decipher the numbers on a digital blood pressure machine and apply them to the patient's treatment there is a need to understand the circulation of blood in the human body. Before we can travel using satellite navigation resources we need to know where we are going. An astronaut may be able to see the destination of the rocket, but until references are keyed in and the whole space team is on hand with all their specialist knowledge the rocket will never be launched. Interpreting the Bible is no different for we need the tools to understand the meaning that the author is trying to convey to us. As the author is God (2 Timothy 3:16) we need to ensure that our skills for interpretation are finely honed, robust and full of integrity so that we do not mislead ourselves or others in the process.

Having the foundational knowledge of how to interpret the Bible will enrich your knowledge of the Word of God and give a deeper understanding of God and His Son the Lord Jesus Christ in whom you believe and place your trust. Having digital resources will enable you to further hone your skills, but unless you know what to search for, those resources could lead you away from the main source of Scripture which is God Himself. This study guide uses the book of Hebrews as a worked example using differing methods of interpretation which the author has himself employed. The added advantage of studying Scripture using one of its own authors is that the student will be more conversant with the book of Hebrews as well as much needed principles from the Old Testament.

This book will give you the ground rules on which to make those robust searches, diligently looking for the truths on which to base your interpretations. Paul told the young Timothy to reflect every day on the foundation of his faith, building on what he knew was the truth so that he could answer for his faith and then teach others.

But as for you, continue in what you have learned and have become convinced of, because you know those from whom you learned it, and how from infancy you have known the holy Scriptures, which are able to make you wise for salvation through faith in Christ Jesus. 2 Timothy 3:14,15

So how will *you* use this book? Everyone learns in different ways: some by rote; some through visual representation of the text; others devour every single word and reference while many more skim the pages lightly hoping to pick it all up by sheer diffusion. The most tried and tested way to learn anything is to read the theory, then practice it away from the desk using the exercises at the end of each chapter. After that return to the theory and discover what more you can learn about your practice. Empower your study by appointing yourself a mentor and discussing each chapter with them. Learn slowly and steadily, page by page. Whether you are a student at theology college or a home maker, this is the kind of learning that will take years to refine and adopt as part of your regular bible readings.

Additional empty pages have been added so that you can use it as your notebook as well as a study guide. Write, doodle, illustrate as you go adding your own interpretations of what you find in scripture including additional references that speak out of the page to you personally. While studying this book spend time confiding in God in prayer. What does God want to teach you that is specific to your life? As you read His Word, so prayer will be one of the indispensable tools which will enrich your study in a personal way.

INTRODUCTION

From the author of the book of Hebrews we have what might be termed a correspondence course with God. At the end of this great book there is an injunction that God will never leave us or forsake us, no matter whether we are facing challenges of great moral dilemma or learning to imitate the faith of those who have gone before. He will be with us as we set out on a journey of learning: learning the method of interpretation that the Hebrews author gave to all Bible readers in his 'model sermon'[1]. The author has not named himself nor his station, because he wants to direct our gaze to one greater than himself:

'Fix your thoughts, on Jesus, the apostle and high priest whom we confess.' Hebrews 3:1

Instead, the author places himself among those he speaks to, one who will inhabit the kingdom of God along with his audience and learns alongside them.

There is an individual and collective effect of Bible study, which is an important factor in a Christian's stability in his knowledge, understanding and use of scripture. Jesus used the illustration of building on the rock (Matt 7:24, 25), a solid foundation on which words should be built. Words alone are unable to give you eternal life, but rather doing the will of the Father in heaven enables a Christian to withstand the storms of life and 'overcome' death and beyond (Rev 2:7). It is important at the outset when studying the Bible to realise that 'reading the scriptures is an art – a creative discipline that requires

---

[1] McKeen J 2020 *The Model Sermon: Principles of Preaching from the Book of Hebrews* Published by Christianity Today

engagement and imagination, in contrast to the Enlightenment's ideal of detached objectivity'[2]. The Bible is a living document with words that walk through our very beings, dividing muscle, tendons, and heart, ripping away at the barriers that prevent us hearing the voice of God. We should not approach it without engaging our whole selves, knowing that we will be changed as a result of our studies.

What is true of the individual is also true of the local church to which he belongs. Although a visiting Bible teacher may help occasionally, there is no substitute for the indigenous grasp of scripture and facility with the Word of God. How often have we heard the missionary bewail the lack of bible teachers out on the mission field? Bible study will lead every person to share learning with the church family, empowering and enabling growth within the body of believers. Each and all should be a Bible student in whatever capacity is appropriate for them.

There is no doubt in scripture that all believers, wherever they are should be students of the living Word, sharing different gifts as the Holy Spirit leads. Moses, a leader and teacher, was all the greater for his deep concern that his gifts might be widespread throughout Israel and not confined to those immediately gathered around the Tent of Meeting (Num 11:24-30). When Eldad and Medad prophesied in the camp, Joshua's jealousy was rebuked by Moses: 'I wish that all the Lord's people were prophets and that the Lord would put His Spirit on them!' Spiritual health means that understanding and proclaiming the ways of God is widespread, not confined to some imagined elite class of believer.

Hebrews is 'a new testament Deuteronomy' says McKeen[1]. Just as the Hebrews stood on the edge of the Promised Land ready to take it, so Jesus, the 'true and better Joshua' (Heb 4:8-12), was preparing to lead His church to conquer the nations with the sword of the Spirit.

Heb 3:13 brings it right down to our level. We are not to rely on our own fickle and sinful hearts but rather 'encourage one another daily.' Constant cross fertilization among the members is in view,

---

[2] Davis F Hays R 2003 *The Art of Reading Scripture* edited by Davis and Hays Eerdmans' Publishing Com USA/UK

rather than any sense of handing down the truth of Scripture. The author challenges us not just to be teachers but that 'you *ought* to be teachers' (Heb 5:12). We have a responsibility to each other and to the Lord, to use the stage of experience in our own Christian lives and the situation of the believers around us, to teach and learn together. But this also means being a student of the scriptures individually.

It should be the goal of every Christian to be kitted out with the ability to facilitate the Word of God (2 Tim 3:16). Here will be found doctrinal stability and the basis for helping fellow believers by way of teaching, rebuking, correcting, or instructing in righteousness.

In the appreciation of the Word of God, it is not possible to stand still. If we make no progress, we degenerate. Through indifference and lack of spiritual exercise, those to whom the Epistle to the Hebrews was directed became 'those who needed milk, not solid food!' (Heb 5:12). They had not always been 'slow to learn' (Heb 5:11), they reverted to this. These are undeveloped and immature believers who wanted to be spoon fed. They were parasitic listeners who would glean nothing for themselves from Scripture. It is my personal discoveries from the Bible that are best remembered, precious to my soul and most effective in practice. I am not to remain an inexperienced milk Christian (1 Cor 3:2), I must be weaned. Weaning starts with semi-solid food, bland and often spat out. But as the teeth grow there comes an ability to chew and acquire a taste for certain foods. In just the same way, as we train our souls to 'taste' and 'chew' scripture so we will learn of righteousness and the difference between good and evil (Heb 5:13,14). This comes through training and experience over a long period of time. In making a habit of searching and using Scripture, I begin to appreciate the taste of these things in being able to discern what is of real value.

We have already said that the believer learns by practice and studies the scriptures to share them, seeking guidance for day-to-day situations, growing in the company of fellow believers in the local church. But the writer of Hebrews gives us the green light to go further in the direction he has pointed. He does not pretend to have exhausted the mine of scripture truth but whets our appetite to continue. In Heb 6:1-2 he lists the principal doctrines which are foundational to the Christian faith and moves on to things more pertinent to his argument. The question to the reader is, have we a clear grasp of these fundamental doctrines? Understanding repentance from sin, faith in God, baptism, the laying on of hands, resurrection and eternal judgement are all clearly pre-requisite in our quest for Bible knowledge. Not that these elements are required in order to study the Bible but rather when these have been appropriated with a solid biblical understanding we must go further, says the author to the Hebrews. To go further is to graduate from milk to the solid food of the mature (Heb 5:14).

In Heb 9:1-5 the author leaves us with a list of features of the tabernacle which he has obviously studied to considerable profit. To enlarge on these would be to digress from the matters in hand, as McKeen[1] agrees that the author should not be carried away with 'providing unnecessary details'. But what Christian should not fail to take the hint and discover the truths to which the author merely alludes? He introduces many characters in chapter 11 and adroitly illustrates facets of faith from each one. Time is too short for him to pursue this further through the Old Testament gallery (v 32). Instead, he does what all good teachers do, and opens the door just a crack arousing our curiosity so that we have to open the door wide, walk through and discover the delights of scripture for ourselves.

The Epistle to the Hebrews does not interpret the Old Testament exhaustively – far from it. But it does range widely over the various kinds of apparatus for interpreting those scriptures. You may have heard the suggestion that only Old Testament passages whose interpretation is found in the New Testament should be used by us. This is 'safe' advice. But it is not what the author of Hebrews suggests and will lead to an unexplored Bible with a weak view of the glorious story of redemption that God has weaved throughout His Word.

Perhaps you have accepted everything thus far in your scriptural learning journey but are unsure of how to learn solid methods of interpretation given the sometimes intolerable and fanciful use of biblical interpretation. Whilst you want to discover truth for yourself, you have no wish to become idiosyncratic, but for the sake of truth neither do you want to get it wrong. Nor did Paul (Gal 2:2). Therefore, take to heart the injunction that no scripture is of private interpretation

(2 Pet 1:20), because, as the next verse says, it is divinely inspired. Does this primarily mean that you should interpret verses of scripture, not on their own, but in view of the whole Bible? According to Peter's view of how the prophets searched 'intently' (1 Pet 1:10) the answer is yes; the whole Bible references itself. You don't want to be 'so slow' in understanding the foundations of your faith (Heb 5:11) nor charged with handling the word of God deceitfully (2 Cor 4:2). Instead, you wish to be someone who always 'correctly handles the word of truth' (2 Tim 2:15).

Hebrews is a challenge to personal faith and practical obedience, an attitude to scripture and consequently to daily living. It is a binocular view on the Old Testament; truth deposited by God in cryptic form, a fabulous original encrypted detective non-fiction book! The Hebrew author writes in original form for this is a powerful first century sermon[1].

Hear the whisperings of the Spirit as you listen and read – especially in the silence of the narrative. Hebrews brings the Old Testament alive and recognises the importance of all cultures, dispensations, individual lives and brings it all together to point to 'Jesus, the author and perfector of our faith' (Heb 12:2). Without the wonderful gift that Jesus gave us through His death and resurrection, we would not have the living word of God to study today.

It is the Holy Spirit that opens our eyes and guides us through the scriptures enabling us to safely interpret that which has been previously hidden. Cowper (1773, Hymn) puts it like this:

God is his own interpreter
And he will make it plain.

The only safe interpretation of scripture is to rely on discernment given by the Divine Author speaking and teaching through Scripture itself. Even then the interpretations will not be a mechanical decoding exercise for we have Cowper's 'interpreter' at our side:

Introduction

'We have not received the Spirit of the world but the Spirit who is from God, that we may understand what God has freely given us...speaking in words taught by the Spirit, expressing spiritual truths in spiritual words' (1 Cor 2:12-13).

Though what we pursue in the next few chapters will be an intelligent pursuit, it is fundamentally a spiritual activity. Wright[3] says that 'it is one thing to have an infallible Book, and quite another to use it'.

God has not hidden His truth away from us in the pages of Scripture. The Bible is a revelation which He willingly unlocks to the seeking soul in which He has also left the guidelines that ought to prevent misinterpretation. This is transparent in the teaching of the disciples by the Lord Jesus. The Lord's parables had wide appeal. His enemies might see the underlying meanings yet be unconsoled by their warning notes and offers of mercy (Matt 21:45). The casual listener gained little or no spiritual value from them and Christendom's reading of them today, and of much else in the Bible, is similarly ineffective (Matt 13:13-16) and compares with the Jewish response (2 Cor 3:14-15). But the earnest enquirer follows the disciples in seeking a point-by-point interpretation of the parables by the Lord (Matt 13:18-23; 36-43; 51-52). These are two typical interpretations of the Sower whose diligence produces fruitfulness, and the wheat and weeds as examples of eternal consequences, both of which are sufficient to establish the principles on which the disciples can understand other parables. On the night of Jesus' betrayal, the disciples are promised that the training will continue:

'I have much more to say to you, more than you can now bear. But when He, the Spirit of truth comes He will guide you into all truth' John 16:12-13.

After His resurrection the Lord gave understanding far beyond His parables: 'Then He opened their minds so they could understand the Scriptures' (Luke 24:45).

Each generation of Christians needs the same careful schooling to

---

[3] Wright J S 1955 *Interpreting the Bible* Intervarsity Fellowship UK

value and use the Word of God from the inspired New Testament authors back to the Old Testament of the prophets and Abraham. One of the grand themes of Hebrews is the importance and power of God's Word through creation, through our hearts, exposing sin and a need for Christ. These are the themes that are evident throughout the whole of Scripture and the author makes it clear that we as the seekers need to embed these themes deep in our hearts. This is the gospel of the Lord Jesus Christ.

In a small area of Edinburgh there is inspiring evidence from the sharing of biblical knowledge amongst a group of Christians across the whole strata of society. Scotland as a nation, has been left a legacy of rich biblical knowledge, now lost in the secularisation of a culture that cares more about its shopping centres than its churches. The latest statistics show that only 2.5% of Scots would call themselves Christians, far less in the housing schemes across the country. The desire of 20schemes (originally founded in America) is to see the gospel of Jesus Christ transform the lives of those living in these schemes through the revitalisation and planting of gospel-preaching churches, led by indigenous church leaders. It is the consistent intake of solid Bible teaching that is vital to healthy discipleship and with that in mind, each believer is paired with another believer to have weekly one-to-one Bible studies. The Ragged School of Theology (a campus of Vocational Bible College, Australia) aims to provide Christian ministry training that suits those who learn best practically and actively.

The concept of 'Ragged' comes from the first ragged school in Edinburgh, led by Thomas Guthrie, a Scottish preacher and philanthropist, established in 1847 in a small room on the Castle Hill. All who were not welcome in other institutions because of their low social status were made welcome. Guthrie's mantra was that 'The Bible, the whole bible, and nothing but the Bible' and the Bible without note or comment...was the foundation of all its religious teaching. This concept is continued today in making ministry training more accessible to all Christians.

These courses are delivered in Edinburgh, Scotland and paid for through donations to the Ragged School of Theology.

https://20schemes.com/raggedschool

NOTES

God Speaks

CHAPTER ONE
EQUIPPING GOD'S PEOPLE

All Scripture is God-breathed and is useful for teaching, rebuking, correcting, and training in righteousness, so that the man of God may be thoroughly equipped for every good work

2 Timothy 3:16,17

There are many occasions when the 1611 'Authorised Version' (AV) has particularly happy turns of phrase - one of these is the perfect completion of the education of the 'man of God' who through his facility with the Word of God is said to be 'thoroughly furnished unto all good works' (2 Tim 3:15-17). The picture in our minds is of a room with everything ready to be used by an occupant. When someone is looking for an apartment to rent, they often want a place that they can move straight into without having to either redecorate or furnish. In other words, they want the apartment available for rent with furniture, fully furnished. Furnishing someone with something means giving or supplying them with equipment that they need for the activities they are going to undertake. Equally when an apartment is unfurnished that person knows they have an inordinate amount of work to do to bring it up to the standard they require.

When we apply this word 'furnished' from the AV to the modern equivalent of 'equipped' in the NIV we can see the slightly different nuance implied by each word. Furnishing a home gives the impression of security, individuality, warmth yet with every piece used for a purpose. Without that furnishing, there is no baseline to work from and the potential resident cannot move in until considerable work has been done. Equipping something, however, has a direct purpose which is more clinical or sanitized although just as necessary. Just like furnishing, it is an active word where the user cannot start to work until he is equipped appropriately. Either word could be used in this context, and both give meaning to readers of the Bible. To furnish or equip someone with the skills to interpret scripture requires hard work, but once they have that knowledge, they can take any part of the Bible and apply it in the same rigorous way to discover the truth. God desires that His Word breathed into being through the pen of earthly authors be understood in such a way as to enable and empower men and women to live like His Son.

To understand God's Word, we have to read it. Once we start to read it, we realise that we need to understand it and apply it to our lives. In the following chapters we will hopefully discover a Bible student who has striven to master God's signposted way of understanding scripture - this person sets the limits of their imagination in interpreting scripture where the Holy Spirit wants them set and will limit approaches and methods to those certified by the scriptures themselves. Their Bible study will bless, challenge and, according to their gifting, will be shared with God's people.

It is helpful to begin with looking at a series of statements that direct the student through the epistle to the Hebrews, analysing it in hermeneutical and exegetical terms. First, what do we mean by 'hermeneutical' and 'exegetical'? Hermeneutics means to interpret or translate. The word comes from the Greek god Hermes who was the messenger of the gods, translating what was beyond human understanding into earthly intelligence . Hermeneutics therefore is the science of interpretation, particularly with regard to scripture. Exegesis on the other hand, is the process by which a student examines a passage to understand it completely for himself. Not all that knowledge will be necessarily shared but the teaching, or exposition, will be born out of personal critical understanding and interpretation. The student may wish to add theological classes to this study to embrace the substance of the epistle as well as the methods of interpretation described in this book.

Zuck[4] is certain that anyone who reads the Bible must understand its meaning before personal application. This is essential and indeed

James (1:22-25) says we must not just read it and walk away, but instead apply it in order to be blessed.

The following statements enable the student to adopt an orderly approach to any passage which he proposes to study. Over the next few chapters of the book, we will look at these statements, examining them in detail concluding with four case studies as a practical exercise to consolidate the learning.

1. Before any interpretation is attempted, the student should become completely familiar with the passage, reading it through many times, probably in various versions grasping its literal and primary meaning. Dictionaries will be useful at this point.

2. Just as the author of Hebrews carefully considered his sermon layout, the student will need to decide with care where their study should start and where it should stop, seeking to include all material which necessarily hangs together. The study then has set boundaries without meandering into unhelpful areas for that subject.

3. Next the student should test their understanding by paraphrasing in as few words as possible the gist of the passage. Putting scripture in your own words enables you to see clearly what you don't understand and where the focus of your learning should be directed.

4. It is probably important at this stage, to reach a decision as to which 'age' the message is directed; is it simply historical or is it prophetic, pointing forward to an age to come? The tenses of the verbs will be a guide, or that invisible knowledge of the order of events throughout scripture. Not only should the student be studying particular passages which have been brought to his attention by the Holy Spirit, but also continually reading the whole of Scripture in order to understand the plan

---

[4] Zuck, R 1991 *Basic Bible Interpretation: A Practical Guide to Discovering Biblical Truth* Victor Publishing USA UK

which God makes known to man, by which he must be rescued from his sinful state.

5. Look for keywords, often repeated, making use of a concordance which will show whether this word is unique to the passage, or is the place of its introduction in scripture. This would make it of special significance depending on where the trail of this particular word leads or its placing in scripture.

6. With this information to hand the student can start to ask what the passage teaches about the Lord Jesus Christ. All of the Bible is directed by God as primary author, towards His Son. There will be evidence of comparisons, contrasts, types or shadows, or examples. This will enrich personal worship and service.

7. It is during this period of study that the student can interrogate themselves on the applicability of the passage as to personal conduct, relationships, spiritual life, the plan amongst God's people, duties as a son and a servant, a priest, and a 'prophet'.

8. Having discovered the richness of the passage, the student can choose to go even further into a topical study, a biographical study, a word study, or chronological study.

9. The aim of the task is for scripture to produce a lasting effect of spiritual value.

10. Never will a valuable study into which the Holy Spirit has led you be wasted. For it will be passed on in testimony, contribute to corporate worship, find its way into writing (the most valuable contribution from studies of Hebrews), or brought to the notice of God's people in a challenge mixed with gracious humility. All of which will realise the glorious purposes of the Holy Spirit. Some believers have brought great blessing by practising this at a personal level within the fellowships where they meet. If you do go on to preach the Word of God then, says McKeen[5]

---

[5] McKeen J 2020 *The Model Sermon: Principles of Preaching from the Book of Hebrews* Published by Christianity Today

preach the text in front of you – if confronting then confront, if comfort then comfort, if human responsibility, then preach the need to repent and believe.

Practical Exercise

At the beginning of this study book, what would you say is the most helpful way for you to study a Bible book like Hebrews?

As you go through the rest of the book, keep your own study methods in mind, re-examining it every now and again, tweaking it as necessary until we return to this question at the end of the book. By the time you reach that point, it is to be hoped that you will have refined your way of interpreting and studying the Bible that will stand you in good stead for the rest of your earthly life.

NOTES

God Speaks

Chapter Two
The Epistle to the Hebrews

'Vision is more powerful than sight' J McKeen

Hebrews is now freely available to us but probably to few of the first century believers. Olyott[6] suggests that it was written around A.D.65 because of possible hints that the temple would soon be destroyed (Heb 12:27). He further indicates that it could have been written from Italy (Heb 13:24) to the Jews in Jerusalem because of the many rites and sacrifices mentioned in the letter. However, for us today it is the best example we have of a Christian sermon that is 'filled with timely exhortations'[7] and therefore is of utmost use in learning to live holy lives. It is a unique guide to interpreting scripture with ample material to equip us to make use of the Word of God in divinely intended ways. Yet it is no arid volume on techniques, for it is applied to a pivotal concern of believers of every century. That is, are we as readers of God's Holy Word correctly interpreting it, so that the truth be lived out in our daily lives? The tools that we are going to be examining from the book of Hebrews are powerful, through which we can feel their cutting edge as one after another in rapid succession is applied to so many Old Testament passages, bringing out relevance to the situation in hand. Kelly[8] writes that 'it [Hebrews] is the finest and indeed the

---

[6] Olyott S 2010 *I wish someone would explain Hebrews to Me!* Banner of Truth Edinburgh UK
[7] McKeen J 2020 *The Model Sermon: Principles of Preaching from the Book of Hebrews* Published by Christianity Today

only specimen of teaching, properly so called, in the New Testament. It is not a revelation given by prophetic or apostolic authority.'

We can liken Hebrews to a correspondence course, God's correspondence course. Because in it we are presented with a way of handling scripture, enabling study at our own pace, and using the individual abilities that the Holy Spirit has given to us. Not only is it our aim to learn how to draw out from any scripture, in a legitimate way, help for our present situation, but also to discover a way in which to apply scriptural truth in practical everyday living of church life and to accurately learn the technique of bringing the truth to other believers. We should seek to interpret passages correctly in their contexts, but, beyond that, to understand the basic principles according to which text of scripture should be applied to its readers and hearers so that they are challenged concerning their personal faith in, and practical obedience to, the Lord.

The seriousness of Biblical interpretation cannot be overestimated. To get it wrong means to challenge God Himself on His holy and perfect authorship of His Word. But to get it right will mean a transformation of our understanding of God and therefore our relationship with Him and His Son. Personal reading of the Bible will enable us to live in the way God wants us to live – holy and acceptable in His sight.

So how do we ensure that what we are reading, and understanding is right? Corporate reading of God's word in Bible studies or in church is helpful because each person can give their own interpretation, but will this just give a Heinz variety of biblical food without robust understanding? Listening to ministers, preachers, pastors of the word is useful because they have prior understanding and years of studying the Bible. But have they remained faithful to God's word? Do they practice what they preach? Then there is the thorny issue of language. Do the present versions of the Bible do justice to the original language and meaning of scripture and have the translations been pure enough

---

[8] Kelly W (undated) *Introductory Lectures: the Epistle to the Hebrews* Bible Truth Publisher Illinois Available at: http://biblecentre.org/content. php?mode=7&item=271 accessed Nov 2021

to mean what the authors meant it to mean?

Here in Hebrews, we have been given a way of reading the Bible which will enable us to remain faithful to the original meaning and a foundation of interpretation for the whole of Scripture. The caveat, however, is that we need to be serious about our reading technique and interpretation of this most Holy of Books.

So where shall we start? Sometimes it is useful to understand the root of particular words to find out what it is we want to know or the answer to something for which we have not yet found the question. We have already examined the words 'furnished' and 'equipped' by looking at common current language.

For instance, several different, but closely related words are used in the Greek New Testament to express the thought of interpretation. Vine's[9] *Expository Dictionary* explains each of the following. First, *'epilusis*, from *epiluo* to loosen, solve, explain, denotes a solution, explanation'. It is used in 2 Peter 1:20, where it translated 'of any private interpretation' in the AV but 'by the prophet's own interpretation' in the NIV. The verb *epiluo* is used in Mark 4:34, where it is translated 'expounded' in the KJV/AV, and 'explained' in the NIV. Secondly, *'diermeneuo*, to interpret fully, to explain'. In Luke 24:27 it is used of Christ when interpreting to the two on the way to Emmaus 'in all the scriptures the things concerning Himself'. Here the AV translates it as 'expounded', while the NIV has 'explained'. Thirdly, the related word *hermeneuo* is used when explaining the meaning of words in a different language and is found in Hebrews 7:2 in connection with the priest-king Melchizedek. The meaning of his name is explained as 'king of righteousness', literally, 'being interpreted'. Finally, *exegeomai*, which means literally to lead out, signifies to make known, rehearse, declare, and is used in John 1:18, in the sentence, 'He hath declared Him' (AV) that is, the incarnate Son of God has made the Father known, both by His perfect life and by His teaching. This word is the one from which we derive our word 'exegesis', our usual word for the full explanation

---

[9] Vine WE 1997 *Expository dictionary of Old and New Testament Words* Nelsons USA

of the Bible text. In this passage the NIV translates it as 'has made him known'. Christ is the full and final revelation of God.

These words lie behind the study of the principles of interpreting all scripture alike, which is often called by Bible students 'hermeneutics' from one of them, namely, *'hermeneuo'*, a word used in the Greek New Testament for interpreting or expounding scripture as we explained in the previous chapter.

Our attitude to Scripture

The writer of Hebrews adopts the essential attitude to scripture which every spiritually minded Bible student should have. That is to view the Old Testament as truth deposited by God in cryptic form, through the use of literal and historical narrative as well as other variations of prose. We can observe his method of approach and interpretive methods for his specific purpose when writing this sermon, and then use comparable methods for wielding the Sword of the Spirit in the challenging spiritual issues which face us today. Stibbs'[10] New Bible Commentary observes that the Hebrews author 'regards the Old Testament Scriptures as full of figures and anticipation of the true realities of God's purpose. Therefore, he continually asks them to support, illustrate and develop his own theme,' seeing the 'Old Testament scriptures as a God-given handbook of instruction.'

Not only will we look at Hebrews and see what methods of interpretation are accredited by the Holy Spirit, and to which He gives special weight, but we will also note that some methods much favoured today in training Bible expositors are used little if at all by the inspired writer. This may put question marks over some commentator methods.

An overview of interpretative methods

First, it would be wrong to ignore what Christians who have gone before discovered when they looked at Hebrews in a similar way to the text that we face, so we will explore this briefly. It is important to

---

[10] Stibbs A 1954 2nd Ed New Bible Commentary Inter-varsity Fellowship

distinguish the details and facts of the epistle (the way its recipients were addressed, who they were and what they needed to know) from the method of applying the Old Testament. This will be a practical illustration of using the interpretation of scripture for a specific purpose. Finally, we will free ourselves particularly to concentrate on studying the author's system of exposition.

Our first major task is to establish why the author of Hebrews felt he could put his faith in the interpreted Word of God and then exercise immense influence in the Church of his day. Olyott[11] explains that Hebrews was written to a group of Christians who had lost their way. They had been persecuted beyond belief by Nero, yet their strictly legalistic Jewish counterparts were allowed to continue with their rituals because the Romans deemed it legally appropriate. Their reasoning was: why not return to the rituals and be left in peace? The comfortable alternative is a human default mechanism, but Jesus did not call us to this way of life. His is the way of the cross and the Epistle to the Hebrews is a timely reminder of God's grace and mercy which brought us redemption through the blood of the Lord Jesus Christ.

An overview of the methods the author uses (and does not use) will follow. Do we quote Scripture in our exhortations as we should? Do we use quotations appropriately in the right context? How do we choose our quotations? As there are around 35-39 quotations from the Old Testament, depending on your definition of quote versus allusion, Hebrews will give a helpful guide.

The Epistle will also give useful guidance about translations of the Bible. Verbal inspiration, biblical chronology, the thorny subject of dispensations, Scripture prophecy, topical studies, character studies, a lesson on Levitical ritual and that fearsome method of typology are all wholesomely illustrated in a beautifully balanced way as the Holy Spirit guided the Epistle's writer. There are dangers in defending a position by calling on the God-given book of illustrations which the Old Testament provides. We will also look at the warning to the scripture

---

[11] Olyott S 2010 *I wish someone would explain Hebrews to Me!* Banner of Truth Edinburgh UK

interpreter which the epistle incorporates. Three Old Testament passages are considered in depth by the author of Hebrews. These will be used as case studies, along with a fourth case study, to reinforce the lessons learned. In conclusion, as in any other correspondence course, we must assess to what extent we have fitted ourselves for the Master's use in handling His word.

Practical Exercise

McKeen's[12] quote at the beginning of this chapter, 'Vision is more powerful than sight', is directed at Heb 11:27 where the faith of Moses was such that he endured the wrath of his previous protector Pharaoh, giving up the comforts of a palace in order to lead his people to the Promised Land. He could not see God, even although he asked to (Ex 3:13; 33:18) but he experienced the presence of God in a way that few have ever done so since.

1. *Write down all the experiences of God that Moses literally saw; those that he felt and finally those he neither knew nor felt but believed by faith.*

2. *How does this compare with your experience of God?*

3. *Read the story below and describe what it must be like to 'see' something without literally sighting that object with your eyes.*

4. *Find someone to tell this story to and then move the conversation around to God and your understanding of believing in something you cannot see.*

5. *Listen to the song by Keith and Kristen Getty 'By faith and not by sight' lyrics and music found at https://www.youtube.com/watch?v=fXB8ihepUpE and reflect on whether your faith is based on what you see, what you feel; what you know or all three.*

---

[12] McKeen J 2020 *The Model Sermon: Principles of Preaching from the Book of Hebrews* Published by Christianity Today

Henry Wanyoike as a young boy, was set for the most illustrious career in athletics. But on May 1, 1995, at the age of 21, he went to bed and woke up to 95% darkness after suffering a stroke. The rest of his sight slowly disappeared over the following years and suffering from the darkest depression, he thought his life had come to an end. However, his mother Grace, took him to the Kikuyu Eye clinic run by the Christian Blind Mission International and the chief of the Low Vision Project helped Henry to find his way back to life, by helping him to knit pullovers. He became self sufficient and with the help of a running guide, he went on to win a gold medal in the Paralympic games in Sydney, Australia in 2000. In fact, he ran so fast that he was outrunning his guides! A blind runner is connected to the guide by a tether on the wrist which the guide uses to subtly indicate, without breaking stride when to turn, accelerate or avoid an obstacle. He then branched out into other events on the athletic track, becoming one of the very few athletes in the world to venture beyond one or two events. He promised himself that he would help other blind people and give them another chance of life as he had been given. Through his prize money he has purchased knitting machines and set up programmes all over Kenya. After his track career ended, Henry set up the Henry Wanyoike Foundation, which has improved the lives of thousands of people throughout Kenya through life changing operations; resources for the blind; setting up schools and annual athletic events.

Let us see the world around us with your vision O God

NOTES

God Speaks

CHAPTER THREE
INTERPRETIVE METHODS AND HELPS

Interpretation is the step that moves us from reading and observing the text on to applying and living it out

Roy Zuck

There are many ways to interpret scripture. Zuck[13] says that often people jump from observation to application, skipping the essential step of interpretation. But interpretation is the most important part of the journey in reading scripture. If missed out, the reader can close the Bible thinking whatever 'is right in his own eyes' rather than the truth of the words he has read. Scripture never changes – it is the infallible, immutable Word of God. It is the reader who changes because the reader is sinful, frail man who will interpret words according to his own situation. Finding the right interpretive methods is key to the personal application of scripture.

Books on Biblical interpretation are often collected together into families. Following Berkhof's[14] *Principles of Biblical Interpretations*, there are the grammatical methods which study the words and structure of the text and then there are the historical methods which uses the circumstances of the author, his subject, and his times. Some

---

[13] Zuck, R 1991 *Basic Bible Interpretation: A Practical Guide to Discovering Biblical Truth* Victor Publishing USA U

[14] Berkhof L 1950 Principles of Biblical Interpretation (sacred hermeneutics) Baker Bookhouse Grand Rapids, Michigan USA

like to call another group the theological method, seeking the spiritual interpretation in the context of the whole revelation of God.

Following the author of Hebrews, we will be mostly concerned with the third family. To the first two we will not do full justice, because they represent the primary steps in any Bible study: the student must commence by being sure what the inspired author meant, and what his original readers understood through his writings. The context of the passage is of paramount importance when reading any part of scripture. As others have said, if you take text out of context you are left with a pretext. Comparisons between scriptures; chronological viewpoints of scripture; geographical aspects; thematic studies; biographical methods; methods with prophecy and hortatory interpretation, which is used in challenging preaching, can also be used in biblical interpretation.

The list is overwhelming, but we have restricted our task to simply observing the way in which one inspired writer tackles the interpretation of the Old Testament. Some students become stuck on one method only without taking the trouble to discover the richness which comes from different methods of interpretation. The writer of Hebrews uses the methods of spiritual interpretation which were suited to the passage and his readers' needs. There are popular and there are fanciful (for instance, the use of biblical number groups *app 1*) methods of interpretation. We may expect a balanced use of the first but no use of the second to be found in our guidebook to spiritual interpretation, the epistle to the Hebrews. We should expect a divine balance on the use of the Old Testament because of the overruling of the Spirit. This is a God given example of the Holy Spirit guiding the author into all truth (John 16:13).

The following table (1) lists the methods of interpretation which the author of Hebrews has employed. This is not an exhaustive list by any means but gives an overview of the Biblical interpretive methods.

Table 1: Methods of Biblical interpretation used in Hebrews

Method of Interpretation	Explanation
Messianic Interpretation (Ch 5)	Jesus Christ, the key to all scripture: Luke 24:27,44; John 5:39
Chronological Interpretation (Ch 9)	Significant order of events and revelations in the Old Testament
Biographical Studies (Ch 13)	Hebrews explores Melchisedec's biography
Genealogical approach (Ch 9)	Acquiring a knowledge of Old Testament family trees
Word Studies (Ch 8)	Depending on verbal inspiration across the whole of Scripture
Topical Method (Ch 12)	The original chain reference is on Faith in Hebrews 11
The theology of covenants (Ch 10)	A specific but important biblical topic
Dispensational Approach (Ch 10)	Hebrews is corrective in our understanding of this interpretive tool
Typology (Ch 15)	Used in a wider sense across scripture, but carefully explained by the author of Hebrews
Prophetic and Literalistic Approaches (Ch 11)	A specific example of which is chronological interpretation
Divine origin of a doctrine (Ch 5)	The ultimate infallibility of God in scripture
The Gist, Paraphrase or Category of a Passage (Ch 3)	The identification of its major purpose; often reduced to a single word summary
Comparative Approach (Ch 7 and 8)	Often in Hebrews, introduced by the key word 'better'
Interrogatory method (Ch 18)	A device for challenging his audience where the writer of Hebrews asks himself the questions 'with whom?' or 'to whom?' Hebrews 3:17,18

One of the most important features of several of the methods of Scripture interpretation found in Hebrews is that they require an overall knowledge of the Bible before they can be applied. Namely chronological interpretation; biographical studies; genealogical approach; topical methods; dispensational approach and divine origin of a doctrine. The author knew his Old Testament and so the Holy Spirit used that prior knowledge inspiring him to go further in his exposition. It should be noted here that inspiration never made up for defective knowledge of the Word of God. The serious Bible student must have an idea of the content of every book or chapter of scripture. This is best gained by continual reading and rereading of the whole volume. Each believer according to his ability will come to their own preferred and effective way of gaining a working knowledge of Scripture.

Helpful Reference Books

One industry pursued by Bible scholars of almost all ages and undoubtedly well known to the New Testament writers, is the commentary on the text of whole sections of Scripture. These are teachers and scholars who offer their own interpretation after many years of knowledge and experience[15]. Most of our bookshelves would be quite bare if not adorned by several sets of these. Now it is strange, but in the scriptures, very few parts could justly be compared to these commentaries. Of the many comments of a scripture on other passages, it is noticeable that these are not intended to be generally informative, but rather they tackle specific points in the development of the author's argument.

The Bible student also does well to have defined objectives, questions he needs to answer, problems to solve, or doctrines to understand. The commentary frequently fails to recognise or address the students' specific enquiry. Furthermore, it is not unusual for commentaries to be the vehicle by which a scholar presses his own theological position. Although textual notes and many informative asides may be picked up from commentaries, the student is often impressed by the disagreements between one and another. He will find few which are thoroughly authoritative and although the learning they contain ought not to be despised, they should be treated as a last resort rather than a first recourse for Bible study. Berkhof[14] also makes this point in his general book on interpretation. If using commentaries, always select those who work from the original languages of Hebrew and Greek as they wrestle with the original meaning of the text[15]. Never be tempted to rely too heavily on them and therefore short circuit your own study of the text. The first step for study of the Bible is the Bible itself.

The Bible student will usually find much more help from a concordance than any other aid. These differ in completeness: from containing every word in scripture to being considerably abridged. They help us when our memory is deficient to find a verse which we have lost. But for this we must have some reasonable idea of the text of Scripture on which the concordance is based. This should be kept in mind when we decide which text or translation of Scripture we are going to use as the main one to read and study. God has given us quite different abilities: if we can do so, we should seriously consider studying the Scriptures in their original languages. If not, we should use concordances for the English reader which distinguish among the various Greek and Hebrew words translated using the same English word, and the various English words used for each word in the original languages. Some of these are more demanding on the user; we each need to use the most comprehensive concordance which fits our capabilities. An interlinear text where the English translation of each word is written below the original text, sometimes makes for more efficient use of concordances by those of us with a good knowledge of the original language.

Copies of the Scriptures with textual marginal or foot notes are of great help provided the student makes himself familiar with the methods of notation which have been used. Newberry's edition of the Bible[16] is one of the best known for English readers, although many more have followed this edition in the last fifty years. Generally, the serious reader of the Scriptures will obtain an edition with parallel passages and some alternative translations in the margins. The value of these

---

[15] Robinson H 2001 2nd ed. *Expository Preaching: Principles and Practice* IVP England

[16] Newberry's New English Study Bible 1970 Oxford and Cambridge University Press

differs somewhat with the publishing house, but many editions are remarkably free from sectarian bias. It is best not to consult Bibles with interpretive notes until a late stage of study as these tend to make us spiritually short sighted.

Although we will return to the subject, we have in English today, perhaps a richer selection of translations of the scriptures than in any other language. For some, this presents more problems than it solves! Not every Bible reader can grasp with the same ease any particular translation. Some of us have a limited vocabulary: more of us guess, and sometimes incorrectly, at the meanings of many words from their context. It is the responsibility of the Bible student to know which translations give a truer and clearer idea of what the original said, for some translations are strongly influenced by the translator's individualistic opinion as to interpretation. Some of our translations are strongly affected by the ecclesiastical persuasions of the translators, and we should at least be aware, if not beware, of this. Some helpfully paraphrase, others produce bias by paraphrasing. It is important to remind ourselves that behind all of them is that 'quick and powerful' Word of God. Doubtlessly the Sovereign Holy Spirit can and has used each and all of these to reach the hearts of men. Yet some will be of more help and others decidedly less to the individual believer (once again, to an extent dependant on the abilities God has given him).

I think it is not unreasonable to suggest that the believer who is intent on gaining from the Word of God and on feeding on the Lord Jesus, will do best to choose which will be his study Bible, and use others to compare with it. This will make sure that his understanding of Scripture is not built upon his misunderstanding of scripture or a mistranslation. In that necessary stage of growing familiar with a passage under consideration it is most helpful to keep alert by reading three or four different translations. Even small differences such as style of printing with poetic margination, paragraphing, discrimination of quotations and italicizing added words intended to convey the sense to the English reader, all help to grasp the gist of a passage.

Still thinking of helps to Bible Study, a high value should be placed on dictionaries of words used in the Scripture. This may be lexicons of the original languages for English readers, or they may even be more tailored to those of us with less formal schooling, by using the words in a particular English translation (with which we must be familiar, or else we cannot look up the right words). Less important, I think, is a Bible dictionary. In this we may look up names of things or proper nouns (names of people and places) and discover their meanings. The names given to people and places of Bible times are usually translatable into English (see Heb 7:2) and these translations are often significant in understanding the Bible story.

However, these dictionaries often lead into byways of Bible background which can be overrated in spiritual understanding of the Word of God. A good familiarity of the whole Scripture is probably the best background for appreciating any particular passage, yet at the same time the geographical, archaeological, anthropological, and cultural backgrounds can give context to interpretation. Key to the use of dictionaries is the recognition that, whilst these details add interest to a sermon they are rarely vital to feeding on the Word of God. In part this is because these studies are still developing and have by no means reached finality. In their present state these endeavours would certainly surprise the Biblical authors and their primary readership, as well as the many generations using the scriptures prior to our day. On the other hand, Biblical authors had a knowledge of background relevant to their subject which they often chose not to unburden on the reader. This was true even where the readers lived in a different country and culture and is comparable with the absence of evident imaginative reconstructions of scriptural situations and suppositions (both of which some preachers indulge in, to little profit).

Digital Aids

All of the above are now available online and certainly do help to reduce the time spent in searching for robust methods of interpretation, providing you know what you are looking for and have an understanding as to the scriptural soundness of online commentaries. Use computer programmes to classify your findings and build up your own profile of interpretation[15].

Fanciful Methods

The scripture stands supreme in its divine origin and power. No human imagination could improve upon it. The Holy Spirit guarded its inspiration and we must consciously put ourselves under His sway to guard our interpretation of these sacred writings. But let us be fully aware that the history of scripture interpretation is littered with human efforts in treating the Word of God (see Chapters 2 and 3 of Berkhof[17]). One of the main reasons for our study of the methods used in Hebrews is to learn the Spirit's own ways and avoid following fanciful theories of interpretations. For instance, it is, of course, true that the letters of the original languages of Scripture have numerical equivalents, but how often has the Holy Spirit pointed to this as a primary method of understanding the Word (see Rev 13:18). Although numbers in scripture certainly relate to subjects, is the widespread use of them (with multiplication and division) directly suggested by the Divine Author as a basic method of reaching his message to our hearts?

Some have seen orderly patterns such as alternation, where alternate lines of scripture offer its own interpretation[18]. For instance, Psalm 14:3 'All have turned aside, they have together become corrupt (first and second lines); there is no-one who does good, not even one (third and fourth lines). Here we see that the first and third lines interpret one another and similarly with the second and fourth lines. Others observe chiasm patterns, an anatomical term describing the point at which the chromosome crosses over itself, inverting the information (chiasma/chiasmata). In theology this word has a similar definition where a thought is developed within a sentence and then finishes with the same thought but in reverse. For instance, 'The sabbath was made for man, not man for the sabbath' (Mark 2:27). In chiastic structures there are generally four points in one sentence. However, Zuck[18] describes the inversion pattern with a similar definition but using more than four elements in the subject and therefore can contrast and compare additional points.

These descriptions of interpretation imply a fairly rigid approach to

---

[17] Berkhof L 1950 Principles of Biblical Interpretation (sacred hermeneutics) Baker Bookhouse Grand Rapids, Michigan USA

[18] Zuck, R 1991 Basic Bible Interpretation: A Practical Guide to Discovering Biblical Truth Victor

grasping scripture which may negate the work of the Holy Spirit in 'rightly dividing the word of truth' (2 Tim 2:15). We have to consider whether it is right to follow one or other method of interpretation but at the same time recognise the work of the Holy Spirit in our lives as we read and study the Word of God. Whatever we do, we should avoid a mechanical interpretation that takes us by rote through a passage where God desires to speak right into our hearts. Later, when we look at four major case studies of interpretation by the writer of Hebrews, we will include his biographical interpretation of Melchizedek. His interpretation sidesteps all the fanciful discussions as to whether his character represents a pre-Bethlehem visible appearance of the Lord Jesus (a 'Theophany') by writing that Melchizedek was 'like the Son of God' (Heb 7:3). The author of Hebrews interpretation consequently avoids unprofitable digressions (2 Tim 2:16).

However, Farrar[19] would tell us that there are many parallels between the writer of Hebrews and unbelieving Jews. But will this background help us in understanding the scriptures? Farrar[19] sounds a word of caution when he concludes that although Hebrews shows its author to be familiar with Philo, 'his general theology and his method of treating the Old Testament as a whole are totally unlike those of the great Alexandrian theosophist.' Philo was a religious philosopher from Alexandria in the first century AD. He was often misunderstood in his efforts to harmonize Jewish scripture with Greek philosophy. So, although Hebrews breathes the atmosphere of a perfect and eternal state which the pilgrim is sure of reaching (Heb 8:1-2,5; 9:24; 11:10, 13-16; 12:22, 37-38; 13:14), is a believer going to be helped in their appreciation one little bit to be told that this corresponds to an 'idea' of Philo? The writer of Hebrews never refers to Philo for authority, evidently does not recognise Philo's copyright and has entirely differing aims and results, despite the fact that Farrer concludes Hebrews 4:14; 5:10 and 6:13 are quoted from Philo.

---

[19] Farrar F 1912 ed *The Epistle to the Hebrews Cambridge Greek Testament for school and colleges* Cambridge University Press UK

Conclusion

The author's subject and his concerns for the Hebrews are his first priority: the method he uses to apply the Scripture is subservient to his purpose which is why he does not give exclusive attention to any one approach to interpretation. Primarily he is communicating truth by way of his Epistle and in doing this he integrates all the approaches, using every weapon in his armoury, each tool on his bench. Hebrews presents a balanced use of many hermeneutical methods, which we should make our example. Some of the popular methods of today (Dispensationalism, and the 'Laws of first mention' which we will deal with later) are employed but without the overemphasis and formality with which we apply them.

Perhaps the most important point to make about the Hebrews author's method with the Scriptures is that while treating one passage, he often alludes to many others. That is, he always seeks to interpret a Scripture in the context of the revelation of the whole Word of God. What a valuable and basic principle this is! And how much misinterpretation and 'private interpretation' might be avoided if we always adopted this approach (and knew our Bible well enough to do it consistently).

Practical Exercise

1. *Choose one method of interpretation and one passage in Hebrews. Using this method unpack the passage so that you understand it in its entirety, with a view to explaining that passage in your own words to another member in your congregation – or your mentor. Use the explanation of that interpretation from the appropriate place in the following chapters.*

2. *Download a digital commentary and compare and contrast your interpretation of the passage you have just been studying with this commentary. Are there differences with which you might agree or disagree and are those differences based upon your personal opinion or truths which the Holy Spirit has guided you towards?*

3. *Revisit your passage and choose two adjectives in the passage. Go to a lexicon and after working out how to use it, note the translation of those adjectives in both the Hebrew and Greek. Does the translation make a difference to your understanding of the passage?*

NOTES

God Speaks

CHAPTER FOUR
DEBT TO OTHER WRITERS

'You diligently study the scriptures because you think that by them you possess eternal life. These are the scriptures that testify about me, yet you refuse to come to me to have life'

John 5:39-40.

It is important to point out that this juncture at just reading the Bible to further our knowledge and increase our intellect has no eternal use. We need to read with intent and personal purpose. What does it mean for me? How do I relate to the Holy God who sent His Son to save me? Do I genuinely believe that He offers me life everlasting because of the death of His Son which atones for my sin? Whichever way we interpret scripture, says Harmon[20], we need to ensure that it points to Jesus in such a clear way that the reader or listener will only see Him and no other, including ourselves. To do otherwise will have eternal consequences. Robinson[21] is adamant that we need to be 'aware of the wide assortment of interpretive aids to us for use in our study'.

Among previous writers Westcott[22] stands out with his essay on the

---

[20] Harmon M 2017 *Asking the Right Questions: A practical guide to understanding and applying the Bible* Crossway Publishing USA

[21] Robinson H 2001 2nd ed. *Expository Preaching: Principles and Practice* IVP England

[22] Westcott B 2nd Ed 1892 *The Epistle to the Hebrews: The Greek text with notes and essays* Macmillan and Co Scotland

use of the Old Testament in his commentary on Hebrews. This has sixteen pages about interpretations of Old Testament passages, giving information on the origins of the common title of the book. Westcott makes the point that the writer of the epistle has an inclusive attitude to the Old Testament, an assumption which would be demeaned if it were necessary to prove 'that there is a spiritual meaning in the whole record.' To the Hebrews author, 'every detail is significant and even the silence of the narrative suggests important thoughts.' 'Whilst the historical truth of the scriptural records is everywhere guarded' the writer's use of it is interpretive. Westcott[22] also put it another way: 'the Old Testament does not simply contain prophecies, but it is one vast prophecy in the regard of national fortunes, in the ordinances of a national law in the expression of a national hope. Israel in its history, ritual, and ideal, is a unique enigma among the peoples of the world, of which the Christ is the complete solution.' Westcott[22], through the eyes of the writer of the epistle, says, 'we know now, with an assurance which cannot be shaken, that the Old Testament is an essential part of our Christian Bible. How the record was brought together, out of what materials, at what times, under what conditions, are questions of secondary importance.'

Westcott[22], a man of great learning, thus came to appreciate the Old Testament revelation with the simplicity and humility which marked the writer of Hebrews. This discipleship of faith and expectancy to be taught spiritual truth by the Scriptures is indispensable to the believer today. In the following pages we do not intend to attempt to establish the historical authenticity, scientific accuracy or even the divine authorship of the Old Testament. We too will assume that word by word they are written for our learning (Rom 15:4) but only interpretation controlled by the Holy Spirit can possibly unlock the wealth of instruction. A person who finds such confidence in the Word of God problematic probably has an even more basic deficiency: they may well have no saving faith in the Lord Jesus Christ and no acceptance of Divine knowledge, authority, and holiness.

Heading's[23] book is not as relevant to our subject as its title might imply, given that it is chiefly intended to be a commentary. Indeed, the use of the Old Testament is said to be 'almost straining the mode of logical thought to which we are accustomed.' Even though this goes too far it shows that our study demands considerable concentration.

There are of course, many general books on interpreting Scripture for every level of ability of reader. They differ too in the degree of infallibility which they recognise in the Word of God. Since this vitally affects the authority of the interpretation and application of the scripture, this is the touchstone to judge the value of a book to a believer. Taking Berkof's[24] *Principles of Biblical Interpretation* as an example, he makes expressly clear what he views as the infallibility, unity, and authority of Scripture. However, in giving the history of Jewish interpretive methods and the schools of methods developed by the Christian Church up to the present day, perhaps he only underlines the need for this study confined to the interpretive tools introduced by the Holy Spirit in Hebrews. Emphasising the need to grasp the literal sense of the human writers of Scripture, Berkhof[24] asserts that this does not exhaust the sense of the Word and that the Holy Spirit Himself is the source of understanding the fulness of the meaning.

While McKeen's[25] book is essentially on the principles of preaching, it does give some helpful pointers to interpreting scripture while ensuring that Christ is the key focus of the Hebrew sermon. He observes that because the actions of Christ have made it possible for us to enter the throne room of God the Father, we are accepted and loved by Him, even although our efforts are often weak and feeble. The discipline of biblical interpretation is not an easy task, one at which we may often fail, be wide off the mark or feel frustrated at our lack of ability. But the Holy Spirit is ever there to guide us onto the right pathway as we seek the riches of God through His Word. 'The risen and reigning Jesus is the truth that undergirds the entire sermon' of Hebrews, as it should be in all our interpretation of Scripture[25].

---

[23] Heading J 1979 *Types and Shadows in the Epistle to the Hebrews* Gospel Tract Publications Glasgow UK

[24] Berkhof L 1950 *Principles of Biblical Interpretation* (sacred hermeneutics) Baker Bookhouse Grand Rapids, Michigan USA

[25] McKeen J 2020 *The Model Sermon: Principles of Preaching from the Book of Hebrews* Published by Christianity Today

Robinson[21] helpfully suggests some of the inherent dangers of topical exposition, where a speaker will take a topic on theological, personal concerns, moral or ethical issues and use scripture to expound the subject. These concerns are that the subject will be dealt with in Scripture over different passages in different ways but often taken out of context which loses the meaning, giving a confused or erroneous interpretation; or concepts may be read into the scriptural account in order to justify a personal position for 'there is no greater betrayal of our calling than putting words in God's mouth'[25].

Berkhof[23] lists Hebrews among the books of the Bible where the knowledge of the original reader and circumstances in which they lived enable us to understand why the book was written. The Jewish community receiving this 'sermon' were possibly considering a return to Judaism because of immaturity (Heb 5:12) and were in desperate need of solid spiritual teaching. However, he overestimates our ability to rediscover these facts with certainty. David Gooding's eminently readable book on Hebrews[26] commences with an imaginary scenario of the first readers of Hebrews to attempt to answer many of the problems of the book: you should decide whether this is a valid approach. Alan Stibbs[27] writes on the passages warning against unbelief and falling away in Hebrews chapters 3 and 5. Harmon[28] uses two simple sets of questions that we should ask of ourselves when reading the Bible: four to understand what we are reading and four on how to apply that reading to our personal Christian living.

Our debt to other writers is immense for they have given of themselves unstintingly to provide us today with an accumulative library of knowledge. Andrew Murray[29], one of the finest preachers and theologians of the nineteenth century in South Africa, considered mission to be the chief end of the church. At the age of 21 he was

[26] Gooding D 1976 *An Unshakeable Kingdom Ten Studies on the Epistle to the Hebrews* Everyday Publications Canada
[27] Stibbs A 1954 2nd Ed New Bible Commentary Inter-varsity Fellowship
[28] Harmon M 2017 *Asking the Right Questions: A practical guide to understanding and applying the Bible* Crossway Publishing USA
[29] Murray A 1894 *The Holiest of all: A Commentary on Hebrews* ISBN 0-883 68-523-X

given a parish of 50,000 square miles near the Orange River and was immediately thrown into the task of preaching God's Word to a community which had hitherto never received any teaching from the Bible. His life's work for the next 67 years was to write a library for the sake of those who became believers and needed to know how to live the Christian life. Even on his deathbed, his daughter Emma wrote as he dictated words of wisdom from years of experience at the feet of his Saviour. The godly lifestyle of authors shows in their writing and while we cannot know the hearts of others we can be aware that like us they are influenced by their humanness. Our desire must surely be that readers and authors alike 'by constant use of God's Word have trained themselves to distinguish good from evil' (Heb 5:13).

Practical Exercise

Before undertaking any kind of study, it is helpful to ask, 'Why am I doing this?' For every single student there will be many reasons because study, particularly Bible study is personal, often private, but always with public consequences. For some it is helpful to write a journal while studying, either to refer back to or to consolidate learning. Others might prefer to write in the margins of the book while still others prefer to doodle their learning into pictures and graphics. Learning is individual, life-long and it matters not how you do it, but only that you do it.

1. *Ensure that you know what kind of learner you are i.e., visual, or auditory. If you don't know then follow this link to find out: http://www.educationplanner.org/students/self-assessments/learning-styles-quiz.shtml This will ask you 20 questions and then give a summary of your learning style along with some ideas to help you learn.*

2. *Once you have established your learning style you will be able to work out what kind of books you like to learn from. The Bible is full of stories, poems, and illustrations in the form of black text. If you have any reading or writing challenges then decide whether you want your Bible and books in coloured text, small or large font and what style of font. Choose the textbooks that are in the most appropriate written form for you to learn.*

Most theological textbooks, concordances and textbooks are in black and white with small fonts. Take some time out to go online and see what there is available to suit your form of reading. However, be wise in your choice, always ensuring that the author lifts Jesus higher than any other, including himself.

3. *It is useful to have at least one textbook to hand either in hard copy or online, whichever is your preferred library. Take your time choosing the one that fits your style of reading and one that you feel you will use over the whole period of your lifetime. It is worth spending the money for a single good bible commentary, and/or concordance. Or it may be that you can be 'gifted' a textbook from someone else's library which has overexpanded or no longer used.*

4. *If you are an auditory learner then listen to the words of Andrew Murray, a gifted preacher from the nineteenth century in South Africa, preaching on the book of Hebrews and the way in which it can speak into the lives of us today, asking us to know Jesus better. Available at: www.youtube.com/ watch?v=XAQzszxhleg&list*

NOTES

Debt to the Other Writers

CHAPTER FIVE
THE POWER OF INTERPRETED
SCRIPTURE

'Do you understand what you are reading?' Philip asked. 'How can I unless someone explains it to me'.... Philip began with a passage of scripture and told him the good news about Jesus

Acts 8:26-40.

The Effectiveness of Scripture in treating the soul

The most profound revelations of a human soul follow reading or hearing the Word of God. There are many instances of people 'finding' a piece of scripture and as they read, the Holy Spirit shines a light upon their soul, and they see the truth of God as never before. A friend of ours studying Islamic Studies in Albania was walking along the road one day and saw a booklet lying in the way. He picked it up and was astonished to read verses from the Word of God. As he read, he realised that he needed to change direction because the words contained all the answers to the questions he had about other religions. This was the truth which was missing from his studies. As the Holy Spirit commands the light of understanding of these scriptures so their application falls heavily on the conscience and heart until our wills yield to His entreaties. Without grasping this vital strategy of allowing the Holy Spirit to speak right into our lives, the Bible cannot fulfil God's purpose in us and with us: we will have no appetite to study it or proclaim it.

The effectiveness of Scripture in treating the soul is asserted in many passages (Matthew 9:1-8; Mark 10:17-23; Acts 8:26-40). Lane and Tripp[30] affirm that God wants to change our souls, our hearts, into His likeness so that we may be more effective for His glory, both here on earth and in heaven. In other words, he wants to change our sinful nature, the way we are naturally born, into a people that 'think, desire, speak and act in ways consistent with who he is and what he is doing on earth.' But this can only happen if we are consistent with our fellowship and understanding of the words that God has given to us. This is where we find the truth and purpose of God and where the Holy Spirit can illuminate His message to us. One of the tokens of Divine authority is that further evidence beyond Holy Scripture is not necessary for belief in Jesus Christ as the Son of God (John 20:30,31).

The Bible is effective for the whole process of conversion and any growth in likeness to the Lord will follow its consequent reading. The author of Hebrews is inspired to state the basis on which he expects the Word of God to affect the reader, and to which he is going to appeal so extensively. In fact, it is not so much an effecting, but more like surgery:

'For the word of God is living and active. Sharper than any double-edged sword, it penetrates even to dividing soul and spirit, joints and marrow; it judges the thoughts and attitudes of the heart.' Hebrews 4:12

The setting of this verse is the will and character of God expressed to man throughout the centuries demanding man's obedience. For us this has been written down so that these Scriptures speak right into our everyday lives. We should pause and wonder at God's wisdom in bringing an immutable written word to a sinful world. It is good to emphasise this by deliberately calling it the Word of God rather than simply the Bible. Books are commonplace and studying in and of itself is without purpose (Ecc 12:12) so we must hold onto the Divine origin of this Word of God. Books can lose their meaning and edge quickly; the author dies and is more often than not forgotten; readership falls

---

[30] Lane T Tripp P 2008 *How People Change* New Growth Press USA

off; obsolescence is built into a book; and despite the attentions of collectors, so many written works have been utterly lost. In contrast, the Word of God is living and as vital today as when it was written. Attempts to suppress it have merely shown it to be indestructible. It has taken on the character of its author living alongside all the social and technological changes of the human race it was meant to reach.

Of course, all this refers not so much to the physical Book with the vast numbers of translations, editions, man-induced diversions, the wear, and tear of each copy, or even the failings of its users, but to the fact that it is the authentic voice of God. It would be helpful at this point to meditate on the fact that the expression the 'Word of God' is identical to the chosen name of the Lord Jesus (Rev 19:13). John 1:1-3 describes the identity of God. Heb 1:2 expresses His task of communicating to us (God ...hath...spoken to us by His Son). It is impossible to dissect the Word, the Son, from the Word He expressed and which from beginning to end directs attention to Him. What limited knowledge of the Lord Jesus we would have without any written account! But could I venerate the written Word and withhold worship to the Word made flesh (John 1:14)? Never, says John, for this is the glory of the One and Only, who came from the Father, full of grace and truth.

Back to Heb 4:12 where it is no wonder that the Word of God is powerfully effective, living, and active. It operates on the soul. We have been conscious of its activity from our conversion and ever since unless we have excluded it from our thoughts. Of course, it is the sword which the Spirit wields (Eph 6:17) as part of the full armour of God against the devil's schemes.

Three main characteristics of the Word of God stand out in Hebrews 4:12. Firstly we have talked of the 'living' qualities of scripture, its indestructible nature, and the ability to speak individually into the lives of every single man, woman and child that reads it. Secondly, it is active in a universal role that God has inextricably combined with the 'Word' who was with God from the beginning (John 1:1; Gen 1:1) right to the end of time and the beginning of a new time (Rev 19:13).

The third characteristic of the Word of God is its surpassing 'sharpness' with a cutting edge greater than any double-edged sword. We are made to appreciate this by comparison with the finest penetrating sword sharpened to perfection before a battle. This is not intended to be a comfortable picture of the Word of God. It tells of its capacity to reach the point decisively to which it is directed by its Divine author, revealing the heart with all its ugliness, penetrating the barriers we have built to hide our true selves from the Holiness of God. When John saw the ascended Lord, whether sending messages to the seven churches (Rev 1:16) or in judgement on the nations (Rev 19:15,21), the sword from His mouth was sufficient to convey the Word of His Will to every subject. Now we read it in the Scriptures of truth; soon we will listen to it directly from His lips.

The author of Hebrews has complete confidence in the unique scriptures he is handling for his readers. They are quick, powerful, and sharp. He knows it from personal experience and time has proved that his application of scripture has affected the whole church. What a recommendation this is for every believer to be a proficient student of the Word of God!

Four examples follow of what the Word of God can do to the perceptive reader if allowed. They all relate to reaching through superficialities, penetrating the qualities and necessities of scriptural truths which we need in our lives to follow Christ. In so doing the Word of God makes obvious distinctions, which our sinful minds would otherwise blend into shades of grey. As the Word of God speaks into our lives, so the Holy Spirit brings about change and we will be more able to discern the biblical truths which govern our Christian walk.

1. Firstly, the power of the Word of God brings about a recognition of what my natural soul demands from my heaven-spirit. Unaided I cannot distinguish my soul from my spirit nor the cravings of each. But to discern what panders to the first and what stimulates the second is fundamental to practical sanctification.

2. The allegory used by the Hebrew author is that of the skeletal system. Soul and spirit are as tightly bound together as joints and marrow, virtually inseparable and excruciatingly painful when separated. In the body they are physically wrapped

round with tough tissue. So it is with the natural soul and the new spirit that Christ has put within me. My spiritual life suffers because of all kinds of alliances protected by social conventions, personal desires, and habits. The Word of God points these out enabling me to be free, but not without the pain of separation.

3. Looking at ourselves we learn the lesson of the powerful Word. Perhaps the most deeply seated, and heavily protected tissue is the marrow within my bones. Today we know something of the vital importance that bone marrow plays in the healthy body. The effectiveness of modern surgery in penetrating even to this tissue is a faint picture of the mighty power of the Word of God to breech the defences of my soul. It is the way in which God lays everything bare, making it accountable to Him.

4. Using the Word of God to discover, analyse, and adjudicate my motives, *judging the thoughts and attitudes of the heart* (Heb 4:12), is perhaps the most incriminating yet positively life changing task possible. The mysterious connections of reason, will, desire and urge are picked out by the brilliant search light of Scripture. We begin to discover that our responses to life situations are governed by the thoughts and motives of our hearts (Lane and Tripp[31]). During this process we realise that it is our hearts that need to change if we are to respond with a godly attitude to our heavenly Father's teaching. He who wishes to teach must be first taught.

All of these processes can work towards the transformation of the soul, the sanctification of the believer and the positive godliness of his living. This is practical doctrine: the operation after the X-Ray.

I believe that the writer of Hebrews had gone through personal experiences of the effectiveness of the Word of God in his own soul. This is why he had such confidence in the power of the Sword of the Spirit as he wielded it through his letter. You can see why he expected

---

[31] Lane T Tripp P 2008 *How People Change* New Growth Press USA

every true believer to have 'tasted the goodness of the word of God' (Heb 6:5). The Word of God is a sensational experience to the converted soul, unforgettable and incomparable. This assumption is basic to the whole direction of the Epistle. The Bible student must have just the same approach.

Divine Authorship

Scripture is supremely authoritative: it is the voice of the Most High God. The human writer of Hebrews makes no pretence of authority, for in the first verse he declares that the speaker throughout time is God. On Hebrews 1, Berkhof[32] says, that even where there is a human author, 'what scripture says is simply ascribed to God.' The author reminds us of this frequently: the Holy Spirit was the originator of Scriptures (Heb 3:7; 9:8; 10:15-17). Indeed he makes the inspired holy men of God (2 Pet 1:21) anonymous (Heb 2:6) unless it is necessary to pinpoint an author to demonstrate a sequence of quotations (Heb 4:7).

The general case of course, is given by the apostle Paul, *'all scripture is God-breathed'* (2 Tim 3:16). Unless a reader of Scripture reaches this conclusion, how can the Word affect his soul? If the people of God recognise His voice in Scripture, how can they ignore His will? If believers, individually or collectively, test their behaviour or doctrine by anything else but the Word of God, how will they discern what is right? It is this ultimate authority of God that has the right to discipline the creatures He has made.

This brings us briefly to discuss the literal fact of the Bible. If God is indeed the Divine Author of His own Word, then who are we to question the literality of what is written down? Tracing the human story through the length of the Bible reveals a creator God who is neither capricious nor vindictive, but rather loving and merciful, forgiving whenever humility and repentance finally overrides pride. It is important to remember when reading the Bible that His 'thoughts

---

[32] Berkhof L 1950 Principles of Biblical Interpretation (sacred hermeneutics) Baker Bookhouse Grand Rapids, Michigan USA

are not our thoughts, neither are our ways His ways' and in fact in every way His thoughts are so much higher than the heavens themselves we could not possibly understand the process behind them (Isaiah 55:8,9). Wright[33] suggests that because the Bible is a summary of the history of the world, and even of all the words that Jesus pronounced while on earth, it in no way dilutes the literal interpretation placed upon every book. This requires wisdom and discernment when studying books such as Revelation which in some chapters employs allegory and metaphors.

This summarisation of various stories poses challenges to the art of interpretation. For instance, Wright[33] picks out three stories each covered in more than one scripture with the narratives at first glance seeming to conflict with each other:

1. The ascension in Luke 24:50 tells us that it took place straight after the resurrection, while the same author in Acts 1:3 allows forty days to elapse between these two events.

2. The story of Jairus' daughter in Mark 5 and Luke 8 is literal fact, while Matthew 9:18 compresses the story, apparently missing out some detail.

3. The healing of Bartimaeus in Luke 18:35-43 was before Jesus entered Jericho and in Matthew 20:29-34 and Mark 10:46-52 it was when Jesus was leaving Jericho.

Do these apparent conflicts detract from the truth of God's word? These only go to show that eyewitness accounts can complement one another and it is necessary to build a picture from several attestations rather than a single observation. It is only when the student of scripture employs sound methods of interpretation that the glorious truth starts to emerge and we are able to learn more about the God whom we love and serve.

As we read His Word, so the sword pinpoints the areas that we need to change and strips away the defences we have built up to try and

---

[33] Wright J S 1955 *Interpreting the Bible* Intervarsity Fellowship UK

prevent God judging us. But this is His prerogative – is not God the judge of the whole earth, Abraham asked. Paul tells us that it is right to read the word to be challenged (2 Tim 3:16) and subsequently to be disciplined. How will the backslider or unbeliever be brought to repentance and restoration apart from the revelation of God's standards through scripture? The privilege of reading the Word of God carries the responsibility of agreeing with God.

The Unchanging Author

There is another feature on which our author must rely. Suppose throughout the writing of the scriptures, God had changed in His essential character, then how could verses be plucked from here and there to be applied to the needs of the readers of Hebrews? This is more of a problem than might at first appear, because, after all, the epistle is the one book in the Bible which, perhaps beyond all others, brings about the changes to those whom God has spoken and revealed Himself. Indeed perhaps a young believer today may find it difficult to identify the God of Sinai with the Saviour of Calvary. The writer therefore returns throughout the epistle to the eternal and unchangeable God in whom his readers have put their confidence. So he quotes from Ps 102:27 *'But you remain the same, and your years will never end.'* (Heb 1:12). We well remember *'Jesus Christ is the same yesterday and today and for ever'* (Heb 13:8) and the Holy Spirit is called 'The eternal Spirit' (Heb 9:14). Here is another guarantee of God's changelessness: about the Son he says, *'Thy throne, O God, will last for ever and ever'* (Heb 1:8). His purposes are in character: *'The unchanging nature of His purpose'* (Heb 6:17) and *'The Lord..will not change His mind'* (Heb 7:21). Therefore the readers of the epistle can depend absolutely on *'the eternal covenant'* (Heb 13:20).

These seven quotes from Hebrews show the immutability of God. This means the opposite of mutable or a mutation. God is immutable, He cannot mutate or change which distinguishes the creator (Ps 102:25-27) from a creation which can and does change or perish. Mackison[34]

---

[34] Mackison N 2020 Christian Doctrine Lectures: Lecture 5 Divine Changelessness - Immutability Edinburgh Theological Seminary, October

says that knowing God brings us into the shadow of immutability which brings us into the orbit of a blazing fire. We are the recipients of this gift of immutability. God has joined fragile mutable humanity with his absolute immutability (Heb 7:17-25). Because God cannot change, He is always ready to forgive us (Heb 13:5b) if we return to Him. We are saved by His immutable grace despite our sin. What a glorious Saviour we can depend upon!

Continuity of Scripture

Linked with this, and as vital to our understanding of Scripture, and to see the use the writer of the Hebrews will make of the Old Testament, is the continuity of the Book from Genesis to Revelation.

There are many senses in which it is wrong to think of the first 39 books as comprising the 'Old Testament' and the next 27 the 'New Testament'. If this were true, much of the justification of the author of the epistle using the Old Testament would be lost and we might be doubtful about putting Hebrews and the rest of the New Testament between the same covers as the Old Testament. The 39 books are incomplete without the 27: the New Testament is unintelligible without the Old Testament. It might even diminish the value of the earlier books to talk about New Testament doctrine, New Testament Churches or New Testament something else, although we know very well what we mean. Is there any reticence to use the Old Testament in scripture meditation, Bible Study, ministry, or testimony? If there is, what does this mean to a comprehensive study of the Bible and what is the reluctance to engage with more than half of scripture?

The writer of Hebrews at the very beginning of the epistle states that God has spoken continuously from the past to 'these last days' (Heb 1:1,2). After the tremendous display in 'the arena of faith', the author concludes 'that only together with us would they be made perfect' (Heb 11:40). Thus the Word of God is put before us with the assurance that it represents Divine, authoritative, and unalterable truth to be handled with reverential humility and honesty. Yes, we ought to prepare ourselves as fully as we can to interpret it correctly and practically.

Practical Exercise

1. *Lectio Divina is a practice used by the early Christians to meditate on the Word of God, experiencing the presence of God through His Word. The Bible Society of Scotland has many resources which use this method of reflection available at: https://scottishbiblesociety.org/resources/lectio-divina/ . Familiarise yourself with this method of reading scripture by meditating on Hebrews chapters 1 or 11. Put yourself in a quiet place and pray before reading, asking God to speak into the silence. Then take one verse at a time and let the words sink into your heart. Ask yourself the following questions: What do these words mean to the people involved in the text and what do they mean to me today? Take notes as words come to you and talk with the Lord, worshipping and receiving from Him instructions for your life.*

1. *Can you think of passages in the Bible that 'live' today? Find a biblical story that makes the Word of God living and relevant. Recount it in your own words and show how it is relevant to your personal situation.*

2. *Study the following picture El Momento, found in the National Art Gallery of Lima, Peru. An arrow has pierced through all the rubbish of life right to the very heart of a person's soul. What has the arrow had to slice through in order to get to the heart? Imagine that arrow is the Word of God. What would it have to pierce in order to arrive at the epicentre of your heart? And what message would it give you on arrival?*

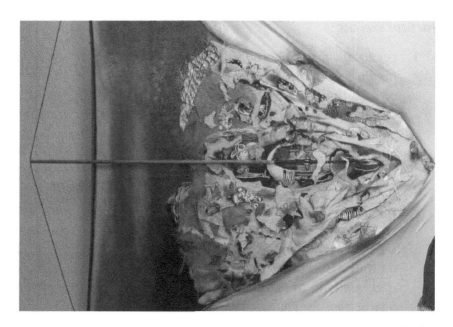

An excellent resource for this chapter is Lane and Tripp's *How People Change*[35]. This maps out a heart route from thorny, sinful responses of our hearts to the blessings of our Creator God who knows us intimately. There are few books that can speak directly and intimately into personal situations, giving the road map which enables the reader to focus on the Lord Jesus Christ, and this is one of them.

NOTES

[35] Lane T Tripp P 2008 *How People Change* New Growth Press USA

The Power of Interpreted Scripture

CHAPTER SIX
QUOTING SCRIPTURE

Let the wise listen and add to their learning, and let the discerning get guidance for understanding proverbs and parables, the sayings, and riddles of the wise

Proverbs 1:5,6

Every reader of the epistle is sure to be struck with the frequency of quotations from the Old Testament. It is profitable to make a list of these, but very soon you realise that some are directly quoted, some are used by the author but not completely quoted, and for others just allusions are made to Scripture. Westcott[36] outlined 24 direct quotations, five-part quotations and 53 allusions from the book of Hebrews. McKeen[37] asserts that the author of Hebrews quotes the Old Testament 35-39 times depending on your definition of quote versus allusion. In the first chapter of Hebrews alone, Kruger[38] reminds us that the superiority of Jesus is paramount, using seven quotations from the Old Testament. But every reader will come to a different set of numbers. This is important for it shows that the Holy Spirit inspired different types of quotation according to the need.

---

[36] Westcott B 2ⁿᵈ Ed 1892 *The Epistle to the Hebrews: The Greek text with notes and essays* Macmillan and Co Scotland

[37] McKeen J 2020 *The Model Sermon: Principles of Preaching from the Book of Hebrews* Published by Christianity Today

[38] Kruger M 2021 *Hebrews: An Anchor for the Soul* The Good Book Company UK

Length of quotation

Long and complete quotations are sometimes used to impress the hearers or readers. This easily distracts or detracts from the object of the reference to Scripture. So, we learn that direct quotations are needed where the words will speak. Elsewhere it is the thought, the incident, or the idea which is significant. Notice that in Hebrews the readers are expected to have achieved such a grasp of scripture that an allusion is sufficient to be aware that it is from the Bible, and they can recall its place in the revelation. The current interpreter must also be aware of the audiences' familiarity with scripture in order to engage them at the right level of understanding.

Another point which Westcott[36] makes is that of the 29 quotations in Hebrews, 21 of them are not quoted in any other New Testament book. The Holy Spirit teaches us to break new ground. The riches of the Scriptures deserve balanced treatment, not confined to a handful of well known and loved passages. This lesson is impressed on us when we think of the considerable use of Isaiah 53 made in the New Testament (e.g., Rom 10:16; Matt 8:17; Rom 4:25; 1 Pet 2:24; Acts 8:32 to quote but a few), yet in Hebrews there is just one possible allusion (11:35). We are told that there is no quotation or perhaps even allusion to the Apocrypha (though check 12:21). Is it remarkable that the author confines himself to the canon of the Old Testament? John Heading[39] sees a different treatment of apocryphal writings. He states that it is the act of quoting a certain portion of the Book of Maccabees (Heb 11:35) which is inspired rather than the actual source of the material being inspired. When there is a difference of opinion it serves to highlight the importance of robust exegesis.

Classes of Quotations

Looking a little more carefully at the quotations and allusions to the Old Testament, the majority are from the Pentateuch, reminding us that this is the Spirit's doctrinal seedbed which we ignore at our peril.

---

[39] Heading J 1979 *Types and Shadows in the Epistle to the Hebrews* Gospel Tract Publications Glasgow UK

The next biggest group is from the poetic books, Psalms and Proverbs. Perhaps this points to the author's daily reading and meditation in these sacred poems. But you can see from his interpretation that it was far more than an appreciation of merely the literary grandeur of these songs. How many stop short of the Spirit's application of these experiences of life and heart! The eye is particularly caught by the words introducing one of the quotations (Ps 118:6). Linking Josh 1:5 with this, he says (Heb 13:6) 'so that we may boldly say... 'What an encouragement this is to use and quote apposite scripture at appropriate occasions! The writer of Hebrews does not ignore the historical books nor the major and minor prophets.

Some of the points we have looked at will be reinforced later when we examine the author's three most extensive interpretations of Old Testament passages as separate case studies, including a study on the life of Jehoshaphat.

Context

As far back as the sixteenth century Ulrich Zwingli (1484-1531) recognised the importance of interpreting the Bible in the light of context. Many might not agree with Zwingli's theological stance but to remove a passage from scripture and teach on it without reference to its place in scripture, cultural significance, geographical placing, the language of the day and many other factors, would be – as he said – 'like breaking off a flower from its roots'[40].

So, for instance, when reading a novel, you would not start at page fifty and assume you knew the whole plot[41]. A verse rests within a chapter which rests in a book which is in the whole Bible. Where does it fit and how does it fit?

But if the writer of Hebrews is economical in what and how much he quotes from Scripture, is he not in danger of taking things out of context? We have all been impressed with speakers who want to

---

[40] Zuck, R 1991 *Basic Bible Interpretation: A Practical Guide to Discovering Biblical Truth* Victor Publishing USA UK

[41] Robinson H 2001 2nd ed. *Expository Preaching: Principles and Practice* IVP England

assure us that he has taken account of 'the context'. The writer of Hebrews never needs to defend himself on this score. As we have already seen, the vital context is the whole of divine revelation. Look how the author takes from its context Joshua 1:5 and uses it (Heb 13:5) without violating the Spirits' intentions throughout the 'volume of the book?' The context in Joshua 1:5 is that God was comparing His commitment to Moses with his commitment to Joshua. Just as he had been with Moses, so he was now going to protect and provide for Joshua. Here the Hebrews author uses it similarly – God is committed to us as believers for the long haul and will never leave us, providing for all our needs if we rely on Him alone. That was the point He made to Joshua some two thousand years previously. Now if it were the author's design or if he had been permitted to reveal to believers a new doctrine, something unusual in the rest of scripture, then any Old Testament passages he employed would have needed to be in conformity to the immediate context.

Even the context of single words is an important part of the interpretation of the whole. A single word says Zuck[40] can mean many different things. Take for example the word *trunk*. This can mean part of an elephant, the boot of an American car; a part of a tree; a piece of luggage; the thorax of a person or a circuit between telephone exchanges. Understanding each word is paramount to interpreting scripture and can present the teacher with a false understanding if the context is ignored.

Quotations from God and man

Westcott[36] deals specifically with 'Quotations illustrating the Person and Work of the Christ.' There are five classes of these which require careful study from the student if desired:

1. Christ the Son of God.
2. Christ the King over His people.
3. Christ Revealer of the Father.
4. Christ the Sovereign Priest for men.
5. Christ the Son of Man, fulfilling all that fallen man could not achieve.

Farrar[42] recognises modes of quotation in Hebrews which he distinguishes from the way in which Paul quotes from the Old Testament. The author may recognise in the quotation the voice of God (Heb 1:5; 4:3; 5:6; 7:21) the testimony of an anonymous author (Heb 2:6) or witness of the Holy Spirit (Heb 3:7; 10:15 and perhaps 7:17).

Hebrews also gives quotations from the Old Testament showing us their fulfilment in the resurrection[43]. Namely, 1:5-13 where the reader is taken back to before creation, the worshipful attitude of angels and the present glory of God; 2:6-8 where the Psalms show us the grace of a merciful God; 3:7-11 the consequences of unbelief by all generations of man; 5:5-6, 7:21 an understanding of the eternality of Jesus as our High Priest.

This brings us back to the relatively unusual feature amongst New Testament writers, where the author of Hebrews does not tell us who the human authors are of the many quotations he uses. He is far more concerned with the Divine Primary Author, than the secondary human instrument. Even a human witness he leaves anonymous (Heb 2:6). The only human author named is David (Heb 4:7) and this for a special reason which we consider later (Ch 9 and Case study A). In general, the writer is adhering to the principle, 'so that no-one may boast before Him' (1 Cor 1:29). But it also conforms with the fact that for whatever reason, the writer of the Epistle to the Hebrews chose not to reveal their identity. It is obvious that what the Spirit has hidden, we would be wrong to try to unravel: it could not be to our profit. It may even be that there was more than one writer (Heb 10:34; 13:9, 22,23) or the author sees no difference between their own spiritual needs and the readers in the 'warning passages'. When the author does self-reference (Heb 6:3,8,11; 5:11) it is not with any authoritative superiority.

---

[42] Farrar F 1912 ed *The Epistle to the Hebrews* Cambridge Greek Testament for school and colleges Cambridge University Press UK

[43] McKeen J 2020 *The Model Sermon: Principles of Preaching from the Book of Hebrews* Published by Christianity Today

The lessons for today's Bible student and teacher are obvious. We avoid intruding ourselves into our treatment of Scripture beyond letting it challenge us on a personal level. And we only investigate the inspired human writers in so far as this does not distract our attention from the spiritual quality of the Word of God.

Practical Exercise

1. *Watch the Bible Project video for Hebrews at https:// bibleproject.com/explore/video/hebrews/*

2. *If you were to use the skills God has given you to give an overview of Hebrews to a group of people, how would you do it?*

3. *Hebrews 9:5b says that we should not get side-tracked when preaching the gospel. Do you ever get side-tracked when you are in normal conversation, and have you noticed that you do the same when preaching? Read over your last sermon or Bible study and circle the times when your notes have drifted away from the main subject. Why was this and how can you learn from this?*

4. *Examine Hebrews 13:5 and write down all the scriptural quotes which match this verse. Are they in the appropriate context and do these quotations allow your learning to point to Christ?*

NOTES

CHAPTER SEVEN
TRANSLATIONS

The promise is for you and your children and for all who are far off –
for all whom the Lord our God will call.

Acts 2:39

A Wealth of Translations

We need divine guidance in the matter of using translations of the Scripture. From every side we have conflicting opinions about the versions we ought to use and those we ought not to use. Readers of Scripture in English must be the most plentifully supplied in the world with alternative translations. Many of them are of undoubted quality regarding linguistic and literary standards. All reflect, to some degree the imperfections of the human translators and are biased by the interferences of their own traditions of interpretations. Doubtless most, if not all, of these dozens of translations have been used by the Holy Spirit to illuminate souls with the gospel and lead believers into paths of obedience and truth. Most of them were brought into being for specific purposes, times and communities and therefore are less or more suited to individuals and uses today.

It must be remembered that the different translations are written by translators who have varying literary genres and writing techniques. The translators had different skills, used different methods and were subject to different editorial referees. They, of course, translated from different versions of the original languages and some are translations of translations. Other translators tried to maintain standards which allow their conviction of the verbal inspiration of the Word of God to come through in their translation. At the other extreme, some sought liberty of expression in English to convey the message of Scripture without any attempt at literal accuracy. These will be an 'easier read' but can be misleading on specific points. It is often the case that the unfamiliar translation says virtually the same as the familiar one if we think over both carefully.

Something which is often forgotten is that very few readers of Bibles in English understand all the English! And this is not just because the meaning of words has changed since Coverdale, Wycliffe, and Tyndale: it applies to translations of this decade too. One of the reasons for this is that the intellectual standards and eruditions of the godly translators whose gifts God has taken up surpass those of the ordinary reader. It is therefore instructive to read the translators' prefaces of several English versions to gain a sympathy with these writers in their task. You might also look at Phillip's[45] book where he describes the task and its rewards.

In any event, wherever a believer has access to more than one translation, there is a decision as to which to follow when seeking spiritually valuable interpretations. The choice of translation will also vary according to the reader's objective – whether it be seeking to memorize the word of God for use in witness or preaching, in gaining familiarity with the text in order to use concordances or dictionaries, giving to individuals of various ages and abilities an introduction to the Saviour, or using the Bible in public reading. In this last case, it will be very important to consider the reading's verbal impact and to take courteous account of the audience's tradition, sensibilities and expectations.

But if it is a case of personal study, the believer will make use of a number of versions in order to avoid being misled as to the meaning of a passage by any individual translation. Reading the same passage in several versions makes the student more alert. No one translation serves to give the breadth of the Word which God Himself breathed.

---

[45] Phillips J 1984 *The Price of Success* Hodder and Stoughton

Instead of being dismayed at all the versions available, the believer should count it a responsibility that he has been better served than any earlier generation and any other language group. Taken together, a multiplicity of translations will serve to take those who know neither Greek nor Hebrew back to the gist of the original language.

We should also make use of several techniques of the translators: which words they added to improve comprehension, but which were not in the original language (and so often are unnecessary additions!). Sometimes marginal alternative translations throw remarkable light on a passage. Of less value, usually, are footnotes where the translator expresses an opinion which is often coloured by his own prejudices. Even typographical differences between editions of a translation aids the student, as when the artificial divisions into chapters, paragraphs and verse are removed, or when the scripture poetry is set out in its double or triple groups of lines.

Guidance from Hebrews

Our approach to translations ought to conform to the direction which the Spirit Himself has given in the New Testament. There has been considerable research into the versions that were being quoted by New Testament writers. For instance, how did the New Testament authors read the Old Testament and what was the language they were using? The student coming fresh to Scripture will quickly see that there are considerable differences between a number of the Hebrew and Old Testament quotations given that we have high quality translations from Hebrew texts. The Epistle to the Hebrews brings this very clearly to our attention and the Holy Spirit certainly does not want any believer to be stumbled by this. If the sceptic thinks that the discrepancies between the Old and New Testament quotations lend weight for his arguments against divine inspiration, it is only to his own loss. Rather, let us say, the inspired writers of the New Testament were guided to use versions where the words and meanings were suited to the Holy Spirits' purposes. John Headings'[46] book is particularly helpful in the

---

[46] Heading J 1979 *Types and Shadows in the Epistle to the Hebrews* Gospel Tract Publications Glasgow UK

way he attributes inspiration to the writer of the epistle in his use of the Old Testament (and even the apocryphal Jewish writings).

Farrar[47] states that the quotations in Hebrews are distinctive in that not only are they from the Greek translation of the Old Testament (the Septuagint) as are so many of the quotations in the New Testament, but they have been traced to a particular version (the Alexandrian manuscript) rather than the one which Paul usually followed. Jamieson et al[48] tell us that only two quotations in Hebrews (Hebrews 10:10 and 13:5) are not from the Septuagint. In the quotations in 1:6,7; 2:7 and 10:5 use is made of expressions which are not in the Hebrew original. Perhaps most well known is the example of Hebrews 9:15 where the author makes use of the meaning of the Greek word for a 'testament' rather than the meaning of the Hebrew word for 'covenant'. Gooding[49] examines the Greek translation which means both testament and covenant. However, covenant has two parties which have to agree, whereas a testament only has one party. So, in the Chaldean version of a covenant, a victim was brought to the two parties who agreed to the covenant, the victim was killed, and blood was shed ratifying the covenant. God altered this ancient covenant to a one-party unconditional promise with Abraham (Gen 15:9-21). This was a shadow of the far greater promise of the Redeemer Christ Jesus at Calvary. But in the testament, there was no victim because it was a last will which remained inactive until the one who made the will died himself. The point the Hebrew author is making using these two translations is that no longer is man part of the promise. The Lord Jesus has made a one-party covenant which means there are no conditions to fulfill except for repentance and faith.

By many measures of modern scholarship virtually all the English translations of the Hebrew Scriptures would be regarded as more

---

[47] Farrar F 1912 ed The Epistle to the Hebrews Cambridge Greek Testament for school and colleges Cambridge University Press UK

[48] Jamieson, Fauset and Brown 1973 Commentary on the Whole Bible Eerdmans Publications

[49] Gooding D 1976 *An Unshakeable Kingdom Ten Studies on the Epistle to the Hebrews* Everyday Publications Canada

accurate and therefore more reliable than any of the Septuagint versions. Therefore, we ought to face the question, is the Septuagint, or even any other translation of the Bible, any less the Word of God than the text in the original language (as near as scholarship can recover it)? Since the Holy Spirit has brought wonderful spiritual blessings to all of us through imperfect English translations, we ought to recognise His sovereign power to use which version He wills for each person on different occasions.

Specific Suggestions

Our study of Hebrews therefore has led us to a balanced view of the rich heritage of English Bibles which many believers have made a source of controversy. But when one particular version has a doubtful translation, the student looking to the Spirit for an interpretation which accords with being led 'into all truth' (John 16:13), can try to mitigate against error by comparing other versions. The following table (2) lists some of the versions presently available which many have found helpful in observing dynamic differences and formal equivalences when studying Scripture.

Table 2: Most commonly used Bible Translations

Version	Date	Comment
King James Authorised Version	1666	Overseen by James 1 of England and V1 of Scotland, who was praised for 'the blessed continuance of the preaching of God's sacred word among us.' It was translated into English out of the 'Original Sacred Tongues'. The English language it employs stimulates more enquiry than any other version. However, many believers are distracted by words they do not fully understand (and may not realise it) in English from this period of history.

JN Derby's New Translation	1961	Derby, a member of the newly formed Brethren movement in the 1830s proffered his translated version of the Bible which was recognised in 1890. He spent much of his life travelling the world teaching and preaching from various versions of this final translation. Perhaps the most challenging part of this translation is the style of the footnotes which makes them nearly incomprehensible. He is remembered thus: He lived in the Bible and recommended "thinking in Scripture." May that similarly ever remain our sole spiritual food, mainstay, and weapon.
Weymouth	1909	Described as a free translation this is the language of the 19th century. It was a compilation of many other European translations from the previous 300 years. Because Weymouth's aim was to describe events of the New Testament in his modern speech it was designed to be used as a commentary alongside the established translations of the day.
Newberry's New English Bible	1970	Newberry was described as an unpretentious student of both Greek and Hebrew texts, exercising a long and fruitful expository ministry. The result of which can be seen in his study Bible annotated throughout with his careful exposition of the language rather than interpretation of the text. Although academic in style, it may be consulted to advantage if with caution.

New American Standard Bible	1960	Considered by some sources to be the most literal and grammatically correct version of the Greek, Aramaic, and Hebrew texts. However, Robinson (2001) declares that while it stays close to the original it can sound stiff and wooden when read in public. It offers an alternative to the Revised Standard Version which some consider to be theologically liberal.
JB Phillips New Testament	1958	An Anglican clergyman, Phillips translated the Bible from the Greek text, putting it into common everyday language all while sitting in the bomb shelters during the second world war. His motivation was the young people in his congregation who did not understand the ancient language of the authorised version. After beginning with Colossians, he was encouraged after the war to continue right through the New Testament. Phillips was a pioneer in modern day Bible translation.
Eugene Peterson's The Message	1993	This is a paraphrase which catches the dynamic equivalent of the original text and reflects the ideas of the biblical author because it is written in contemporary language. It follows the common language of the day in which the New Testament was mostly written so that ordinary people could understand it. This is the language of stories and parables, as Peterson described it – he stood at the border of two languages, biblical Greek, and everyday English, translating it into the right words for men and women to understand and believe.

New Living Translation	1996	The translators' aim was to ensure that the meaning of the text is readily apparent to the contemporary reader with immediacy, while at the same time remaining faithful to the ancient texts. A second-generation text was produced in 2004 to ensure the ongoing contemporary quality of this translation.
New International Version	1973	The NIV searches for the middle ground between allegiance to Hebrew or Greek and a sensitive feel for style (Robinson 2001). It was written by over 100 interdenominational, international scholars working directly from Hebrew, Aramaic, and Greek texts. The goal of the committee was to ensure the text would have clarity and literary quality suitable for public and private reading, teaching, preaching, memorising, and liturgical use. They held to the authority and infallibility of the Bible as God's Word in written form.
The Bible for Everyone A New Translation by Goldingay and Wright	2018	Two faithful Bible scholars have joined together to produce an easy to read Bible translation, using the Hebrew and Aramaic works rather than a paraphrase. Goldingay quotes Tyndale as his mantra for preparing a version of the Old Testament for everyone, while Wright takes Pentecost as his reason for translating the New Testament into a language for all peoples. Maps and diagrams are littered throughout the text and each book carries a basic exposition of its aim and reason for being in the canon of Scripture.

Using different translations helps understand the broad context of the passage. When reading, note your own personal difficulty in understanding a particular passage which may become clearer with each translation. If not, then refer to the commentaries of your choice to see if they agree on an exposition of the passage. There may be differences of opinion amongst the translations which is why having a

Translations

basic understanding of the original texts in Greek or Hebrew is helpful.

There appears to be still a financial attraction in publishing Bibles, although it is difficult to justify the number of English versions which have appeared in the last seventy plus years. The Bible student needs to resist the temptation to buy each new version that is published unless he is certain of making profitable use of it. The solution that some adopt is to purchase one of the numbers of parallel versions which are available with five or more translations side by side. Admittedly they are unwieldy but are more convenient for comparative study than the separate volumes. A convenient little volume on these lines just for Hebrews is Sprent[50] which compares four translations.

Online versions of the Bible abound including http://www.biblecc.com/ which holds 34 versions of the Bible, a Lexicon, Strong's Commentary, and many other facilities. Another similar free version is https://www.e-sword.net/ which is easily downloaded onto home computers and also has maps and reference points with commentaries.

Heading[51] challenges the Bible student not to scour translations in order to find words which fit personal ideas or philosophies. The Word of God is inspired by the author of creation, and it is the Holy Spirit that directs our interpretation, enabling us to be taught and to teach (2 Timothy 3:16,17). In using different translations this facility allows the student to deepen an understanding of the breadth of knowledge that the Holy Spirit has brought to Biblical interpreters and on which we can build our own awareness and appreciation rather than justify individual worldviews. Because we recognise the writings of Scripture as the inspired Word of God, even more must we be careful to quote scripture accurately.

---

[50] Sprent J 1892 Gleanings in the Hebrews The Witness Glasgow Scotland

[51] Heading J 1979 *Types and Shadows in the Epistle to the Hebrews* Gospel Tract Publications Glasgow UK

Practical Exercise

1. *Take three different translations (including a paraphrase) and read the introduction from the translators of each edition noting their reasons for undertaking this particular translation.*

2. *Using these translations, observe the differences in Hebrews chapter 9:15-28 noting the discrepancies and the slightly different nuances that are employed for the sake of translation. Discuss the difference between the words 'testament' and 'covenant'.*

3. *Familiarise yourself with other translations of the Bible and decide which ones will suit your teaching style and will be best used by those you are teaching.*

4. *Search the internet for a reliable, user-friendly online site for parallel translation study.*

5. *Choose for yourself a translation that suits your style of reading for your own personal daily reading of scripture.*

NOTES

Translations

CHAPTER EIGHT
WORD STUDIES

'Meaning does not come from words alone' Robinson

Words and Verbal Inspiration

Zuck[52] describes all words as having four driving influences: Etymology, usage synonyms and antonyms, and context. Etymology is the root development of the word dependant on its culture and language of origin. Usage is how that same word is used by the author at the time of writing. Zuck[52] gives many helpful illustrations of various words that have been developed over centuries which take on an entirely different meaning from the original. Words having the same meaning (synonyms) and having the opposite meaning (antonyms) enable the reader to determine shades of meaning differing from the exact or near opposite. Finally, the context of a word is essential for understanding the whole passage. Zuck[52] divides this into the immediate context of the sentence; the context of paragraph or chapter; the Bible book in which the word occurs; parallel passages elsewhere in the Bible and the entire Biblical context.

The study of the words of Scripture is a sterile pursuit unless it is linked with a belief in the verbal inspiration of the Bible. That is, that the Divine authorship of the Bible is evident, from the scale of the whole volume down to the choice of the individual Hebrew or Greek word.

---

[52] Zuck, R 1991 *Basic Bible Interpretation: A Practical Guide to Discovering Biblical Truth* Victor Publishing USA UK

Indeed, it is difficult to see how it could constitute Holy Scripture if its smallest parts were not circumscribed by Divine choice. This obviously applies to the great words of Christian doctrine which are often not uncommon words but are invested with wonderful new meaning to suit the Divine purpose, such as the word 'rest'.

The word 'rest' means to cease work or movement in order to relax, sleep or recover strength. However, when Jesus talks about rest it is not the absence of external movement, but rather a deep-seated peace of the soul (Matthew 11:29). Hebrews describes the lack of 'rest' as an everlasting punishment for those who are disobedient to God (Hebrews 3:11;18). But the opposite is true for those who receive this eternal rest as a gift from God based upon His own rest from creating the perfect world (Gen 1:3). Traub[53] states that this is one of the major themes in Hebrews, where the author uses the concept of rest, appearing ten times in Hebrews, as a gift from God for holding on and persevering in the faith. God's 'rest' is the perfect state that the world was in when He created it in the beginning and where people return to when they believe in Him both now and in eternity.

You can see then that this use of a common everyday word has been given a Godly purpose which takes on a completely new meaning when examined in the light of the whole of Scripture.

Hebrews and Word Studies

A few examples from Hebrews will serve to make this point where the interpretation of an Old Testament passage rests upon a single word. Consider the words 'all' in Heb 2:8 ('everything' NIV); 'today' in 3:7; 3:13; 3:15 and 4:7; 'speaketh' in 12:24 ('speaks' NIV); 'once more' (Heb 12:26,27). Jamieson et al[54] writes (assuming Paul to be the author of Hebrews) 'mark how verbal inspiration is proved in Paul's argument leaning wholly on one word' which may only occur once in the Old Testament. In case studies later on, we will examine the

---

[53] Traub W 2021 'How to interpret and apply the OT today' Lecture 6 on Hebrews Edinburgh Theological Seminary

[54] Jamieson, Fauset and Brown 1973 Commentary on the Whole Bible Eerdmans Publications

author using the method of word study.

To employ this method of word interpretation it is helpful to be acquainted with Bible study aids, leading back to the original text of scripture in order to get as close as possible to the original meaning of words. These will include interlinear Bibles (with English beneath the words of the original); Hebrew and Greek Bible concordances; dictionaries and lexicons. Learning the original languages of the Bible such as Greek, Hebrew and Aramaic are the most helpful aid to interpretation, however this is not always possible which is why lexicon aids enable the student to sidestep the necessity of language learning. Although we should respect the serious student who has this knowledge enabling that greater precision in interpretation.

Word Studies in Translations

From what we considered in the previous chapter, it is clear that we could not rely on interpretations based on the particular word used in a translation, the repetition of a translated word, or a unique word in the translation. These are the textual methods we would expect only to use to interpret the passage in the original. To claim that interpretations based on the words of a particular translation are reliable, would be to claim inspiration at a level which is unwarranted. This is in contrast with claims for the epistle of Hebrews, which because of its conformity to the rest of the Bible has been unquestionably and correctly accorded a place in the canon of Scripture. Only in the Hebrew author's case are we willing to accept that this reliance on the words from the Septuagint translation, which are at variance with the original Hebrew, is reliably due to the Holy Spirits' inspiration. The rest of the time it appears that the author used the original Hebrew which was sufficient for the Spirit's purpose.

Choice of Words in Hebrews

It is possible to see how the writer of Hebrews took special care of words, not only those quoted and interpreted with such great effect from the Old Testament, but also his own choice in writing the epistle. Farrar[55] lists the occasions when it is thought that the writer employed a play on words, for instance:

- Heb 1:2: 'in the last days' which when compared to other references (1 Peter 1:20; 1 John 2:18 Jude 18) could mean either the entire church age or the final days of the Church Age[52].

- 2:8 Here the Psalmist is saying that 'everything' has been subjected to God, but the Hebrews author refutes that. In a single word the author describes the exaltation of Jesus as Lord and Saviour because His death has brought this about, but the process of Jesus' representation on our behalf, reigning in heaven is still ongoing until all things are completed.

- 5:14: the word 'mature' is used here in relation to the physical growth of a child into adulthood, gradually preferring solid food to milk. What the author is referring to is that we too as Christians should prefer the 'solid food' of spiritual learning, rather than turning away from the challenge of thinking about our faith, as Wright[56] puts it.

- 7:3: Melchizedek was a priest 'forever' yet was obviously a mortal being (Gen 14:18). Because no one knows his genealogy, birth or death, the Hebrews author uses this unknown priest of Salem as an analogy to describe the immortality of the High priestliness of the Son of God.

- 7:19: 'A better hope' describes the essential leap mankind has been given between our inability to obey the law and the redemption given to us by Jesus on the cross.

- 7:22-24; 8:7,8: 'A better covenant' puts a guarantee on the word 'better', because Jesus Himself has become the bridge between God and man.

- 10:29: Here the Hebrews author uses the word 'trampled' to

---

[55] Farrar F 1912 ed The Epistle to the Hebrews Cambridge Greek Testament for school and colleges Cambridge University Press UK

[56] Wright T 2003 *Hebrews for Everyone* Published by Society for Promoting Christian Knowledge UK

describe the significant and dangerous rejection when man turns away from God, particularly if he has previously heard and understood the way of salvation.

- 10:34-38: Once again the word 'better' is used but this time in conjunction with possessions. For those who lose everything for the sake of Christ the everlasting riches gained in heaven are far greater than this world could ever give.

- 11:27: The Hebrew author cites Moses who 'saw Him who is invisible'. The sentence here employs an oxymoron (where apparently contradictory terms appear together) to show the enabling aspect of faith which transcends all earthly values.

- 13:14: 'An enduring city' gives us a glimpse of what is to come because the only thing that lasts in this life is our relationship with God and our service to Him.

Keywords

Yet another way to impress ourselves with the word-by-word treasures of scripture is by looking for key words in a passage. This is the word on which the argument of the passage hinges, and it is often repeated several times. When we check all the references to the original word, a good concordance will show that the Greek or Hebrew word is used quite sparingly in other parts of Scripture (or maybe nowhere else). The epistle of Hebrews amongst the New Testament books has a comparatively large number of words which are not found elsewhere. For instance, coming freshly to the Epistle, a reader is soon struck with the word usually translated 'better' which is found 18 times in the New Testament, and 13 of these are in this one book. Comparisons of people and events with the Lord Jesus feature as one of the most important strands in the epistle and prove that the Lord is surpassing all (Heb 8:6). The frequency of the word 'blood' in Heb 9 and 10 will prove key for interpreting these chapters.

Prepositions and a Warning

Word studies can be pursued profitably even by looking at some of the smallest words, such as prepositions. These are treated rather carelessly by translators, but the Spirit has been most definite to direct us in a godly way with regard to the great doctrines. The notes in the Newberry[57] edition of the Bible has a useful explanation of the relationships between the prepositions. It is easy to see how a student can become stuck on using just one method of approaching scripture such as word studies: however, our concern is that the Bible student will balance the use of all the methods he can bring to studying a scripture.

Figures of Speech

The language of the Bible was generally written in the common language of the people so that they could readily understand it. This includes figures of speech, of which many are used frequently in Hebrews. In our language we use figures of speech every day, such as 'it's raining cats and dogs'. This does not mean that cats and dogs are falling from the sky: it is a figure of speech and may be understood as comparing the high population of cats and dogs in Britain to the amount of rain falling out of the sky. Alternatively, it might be a mispronunciation of the Greek term *cata doxa* meaning 'contrary to experience or belief'. Or again, it could come from an obsolete English term *catadupe* which means cataract or waterfall.

Whatever its origins, this figure of speech has transcended both language evolution and geographical boundaries. Remove figurative speech from the Bible says Zuck[58] and you have lost the living spirit which moves across its pages, because this is how God speaks to us – in our language. The Bible student is required to differentiate between strict literalism and cultural figures of speech.

Zuck[58] gives a list of reasons for using figures of speech: they add colour and vividness; they make abstract or intellectual ideas more concrete; aid in retention; abbreviate an idea and encourage reflection. The Hebrews author employs the same method of writing using figurative speech as writers have throughout the centuries. For instance:

---

[57] Newberry's New English Study Bible 1970 Oxford and Cambridge University Press

[58] Zuck, R 1991 *Basic Bible Interpretation: A Practical Guide to Discovering Biblical Truth* Victor Publishing USA UK

2:1: 'Drifting' generally applies to a ship that has slipped its anchor, or never had an anchor in the first place. But here the author has used it to its full benefit stating later (6:19) that our hope in Christ is an anchor. He is obviously not envisaging a literal anchor tied around our waists but rather that our hope in Christ is as firm as the anchor that holds a huge ship in one place.

3:6: Here we as believers in Christ are described as 'His house' not because we are made of bricks and mortar but because the idea of a house is used elsewhere in the Bible (Ps 127:1) describing the solid unity of Christians as they work together in different roles but all for the same purpose.

5:12: 'You need milk not solid food!', the author to the Hebrews pithily remarks. Exasperated he resorts to figurative language in order to bring them to their senses for nobody likes to be reminded of their immaturity.

Analogy and Metaphors

A metaphor is a word or phrase which is used to describe an object, idea, or action suggesting a resemblance or analogy[59]. So, for instance describing the voice of the Lord as a thundering cataract (Psalm 29:3) is obviously not saying that it is a huge waterfall, but rather a very loud voice that could make a person feel as if they were drowning. The striking use of metaphor is typical of Hebrew poetry wherever we find it throughout scripture. Because Hebrew poetry is written in duplicate syntax, we often have two metaphors just to reiterate the point. When an author is trying to describe an object of which we have no prior knowledge, employing metaphors enables the reader to form an image that is recognisable to their world view. Studying these metaphors from scripture give us a much deeper and richer understanding of our multi-faceted God.

To interpret a metaphor, you must first understand the picture of the metaphor itself. What picture is being illustrated and how does it fit with your own understanding of that picture? If you don't understand

---

[59] Wright J S 1955 Interpreting the Bible Intervarsity Fellowship UK

the picture, then you will not understand the analogy that the author is making. Once you understand the picture to your satisfaction, it is time to look at the object or idea that the author is trying to convey. How does it fit into the context of the passage and what application is the author making to the reader's life? Conveying truths about God in a way that we as humans can understand is almost impossible says Wright[59]. So anthropomorphic (humanlike) or metaphorical language is employed. In other words, the reader is challenged to think of ways in which the truths of scripture resemble those objects described[58].

Stories

Jesus himself used stories, taking real life situations that people resonated with and applying them to his new teachings which were to change the world. Jesus did not have to study theology in order to understand the foundation of his faith. The world, the universe, creation, and God were in fact His own story. We on the other hand, need to study and first understand what He is saying to us in order to find the story and apply it to our life.

In Hebrews 7:1 we find the author employing the use of the story of Melchizedek, a King and Priest in the city of Salem (Jerusalem), who Abraham met while on a desert campaign. This story gives the author plenty of information with which to show his readers similes and metaphors to illustrate his point.

McKeen[60] points out that when describing a salient point from scripture we too should use stories as illustration as 'this is necessary and biblical practice but only use them after the student has reached a proper understanding and explanation.'

Practical Exercise

1. *The following three descriptions are found in Hebrews. Describe them in detail and apply the principle of interpreting a metaphor or simile to understand both the context and application of the passage to modern day understanding:*

---

[60] McKeen J 2020 *The Model Sermon: Principles of Preaching from the Book of Hebrews* Published by Christianity Today

- *Hebrews 1:10-12 'a garment and a robe'.*
- *Hebrews 4:12-13 'a double-edged sword...dividing joints and marrow'.*
- *Hebrews 5:11-14 'milk and solid food'.*

2. *'Rest' has been described in this chapter as a word used in common language taken by divine authorship and given a new meaning. Find a similar common word in the Book of Hebrews that has been given Godly significance and describe both the common and scriptural understanding.*

3. *Find the 'story' in Hebrews 6:7-8 and note down the application for the reader of today.*

NOTES

Word Studies

CHAPTER NINE
CHRONOLOGY

You see, at just the right time, when we were still powerless, Christ died for the ungodly.

Romans 5:6

Chronology

In creation, God provided a clock for the world He had made (Gen 1:5,14). God Himself stops that clock (Rev 10:6; 20:11) when there must be no more delay or when time has no significance. Consequently, many events which the Holy Spirit has recorded in Scripture, and even the order of writing books, are in historical sequence rather than chronological order. Much of scripture is literal history, authentic happenings on which we are able to rely giving our faith a solid foundation.

Chronological Sequence in the Bible

The Bible student needs to be familiar with the order of both writing and Scripture history. Not only does this enable the student to grasp and marvel at the unfolding of the revelation of God throughout the Word, but also as an aid to remembering the place of an event in its time context. In various ways this knowledge is also an aid to Scripture interpretation.

Using chronology to interpret Scripture

One important way in which chronology is often employed is that it directs us to the first occasion on which a word is used, or an event took place. This 'school' of interpretation describes this chronological method as 'The law of first mention.' Certainly scripture, not unusually, has an explanation on the first occasion something is broached. The origin of a doctrine in scripture will be especially significant as well as the circumstances surrounding that first mention. This underlines the special value to the interpreter, for instance, of the book of Genesis - which means the 'beginnings.' While of some value, this approach should not become rigid and inflexible, as the 'law of first mention' can make truth mechanical preventing the student from dependence on the Holy Spirit's guidance to lead him into 'all truth.'

We have already noticed that the writer to the Hebrews used the Pentateuch extensively. Consider his allusions to creation. As there was no man to witness the event, our knowledge of God as Creator (Heb 1:2,10; 11:1) including His verbal command of the world's beginnings (Heb 11:3) must rest solely on faith. The intended place of man in that creation and his actual place are drawn from the seedbed of Genesis (Gen 1:26-28; linked with Ps 8; Heb 2:6-8). The sanctified seventh day after the work of creation (Gen 2:2,3) was seen as the origin of the rest of God (Heb 4:3,4). The first time blood is mentioned in relation to the blood of Abel, led to the author's comparison and contrast with the blood of Jesus (Gen 4:10; Heb 12:24).

An example of a more strictly chronological approach employed by the Hebrew author is found in Hebrews 4:7-9 which we will study more closely later in a case study. The argument here hinges on the fact that Joshua preceded David in the history of Israel, so that what David wrote can be said to supersede the events and pronouncements of Joshua's day.

Genealogy

A particularly important way in which the Scriptures mark the passage of time is by the generations in significant families (note Matt 1:17). Of course, the study of Bible genealogies can be a sterile pursuit (1Tim 1:4; Tit 3:9) if they are not used to point the student to the Lord Jesus and Paul warns about the inconclusive futility of such investigations. However, because the Holy Spirit has set aside a fair proportion of scripture to give us these family trees the Bible student needs to give them appropriate attention.

Family relationships and traditions have profound effects on the spiritual development of men and women. Think for instance, of the significance of recording the mothers of so many of the Kings in the Old Testament. Were these women not major influences on the behaviour of their sons? Unlike today, the family relationship indicated their office in Israel and the location of their inheritance or home territory. Jacob and Moses were aware of the importance of their family relationships and the Divinely determined futures of the tribes. Thus, they were allowed to reveal the prophetic implications of these tribes (Gen 49:1-28; Deut 33). This provides an understanding of many things throughout the rest of Scripture particularly with regard to Hebrews as the Holy Spirit illustrates the value of the genealogical approach. 'For it is clear', he writes (although this will be understood only by the believer who knows the Old Testament) 'that our Lord descended from Judah and, in regard to that tribe, Moses said nothing about priests' (Heb 7:14; 7:5,6).

The most important chronology that we have inherited as humans is the narrative given to us by the One in whose image we are made and who sustains life on earth. He it is who has given us the whole account from the beginning of earth (Gen 1:1) to the very end of earth as we know it (Rev 6:12-14). The Lord speaks to John out of the vision of the end of all time and tells him that he is coming soon with many eternal rewards for those who have persevered and endured hardships for the sake of the gospel (Rev 2:3). Jesus is the ultimate beginning and end of the earthly time He allots us, but also the glorious beginning of the new heaven and new earth where He will always be present.

Practical Exercise

1. *Make out a timetable of events from the time that Amos began to prophesy in 760 BC until Jerusalem was destroyed in 586 BC.*

2. *Compare the chronology of events in Genesis 1-3 to the sequence of events in Revelation 6 as the first six seals of the scroll are unlocked.*

3. *Examine your own family tree and see if there is any evidence of a Christian heritage, remembering that Timothy valued his grandmother Lois (2 Tim 1:5) for all that she taught him. What values and principles have you inherited from your family? How can you pass on Christian values and principles to others in your family?*

NOTES

God Speaks

CHAPTER TEN
THE CASE FOR DISPENSATIONS

In the dispensations God has demonstrated every possible means of dealing with man. In every dispensation man fails and only God's grace is sufficient.

Lewis Chafer

A method of Biblical interpretation which Hebrews demonstrates very clearly, is the dispensational approach where the student must decide to which stage in the progressive revelation of God any particular passage belongs. Dispensational theology is described by Catchpole[61] as a system that views the whole of Scripture and history with several ages united in the message of the Bible. It has always been God's sovereign prerogative to order His dealings with men. At each stage of His revelation, He has given clear guidance to men as to His requirements for their relationship with Him. A clear exposition and defence of dispensationalism is to be found in Dispensationalism Today[62] and also Vlach's essay on the theology of dispensationalism (https://www.thegospelcoalition.org/essay/dispensational-theology/).

---

[61] Catchpole R 2021 Dispensational Theology (1) Lamp and Light The Society for Distributing Hebrew Scriptures January/February

[62] Ryrie C 1965 Dispensationalism today Moody Press

[63] Catchpole R 2021 Dispensational Theology (2) Lamp and Light The Society for Distributing Hebrew Scriptures March /April

The word dispensation means an economy, an administration or stewardship[63]. The dispensations described here show how God reveals Himself in administering and fulfilling the plan He has for the world He created. It appears that in each dispensational age man is given a new responsibility then tested but ends in failure and divine judgement.

Chafer[64] defines dispensationalism as 'a stage in the progressive revelation of God constituting a distinctive stewardship or rule of life.'

Zuck[65] describes dispensational theology as being grounded in two concepts:

1. There is a definite distinction between the church and Israel.

2. The primary purpose of God's plan is to bring glory to Himself (Eph 1:6,12,14).

These two tenets underpin five dispensations[65], or seven according to Catchpole[61] in Scripture. All seven are noted here giving credence to both authors.

a) The dispensation of Eden or innocence – where the simplicity of the law of God was a single command, 'You must not eat of the fruit of the tree of the knowledge of good and evil' (Genesis 2:17). It was in creation that God revealed His person and power both in terms of the world and making man in his image.

b) The dispensation of Pre-Mosaic law or conscience – God dealt with individual men in their knowledge of good and evil. This God given conscience extends to today as seen in Romans 2:14-16.

c) The dispensation of human government – God gave Noah a promise of life as he left the ark and a covenant that demanded responsibility from Noah and the succeeding generations. This secured the sanctity of life because man had been made in the

---

[64] Chafer L 1974 Revised by Walvoord J Major Bible Themes Zondervan Press USA

[65] Zuck, R 1991 *Basic Bible Interpretation: A Practical Guide to Discovering Biblical Truth* Victor Publishing USA UK

image of God (Genesis 9:1-17).

d) The dispensation of promise – the Abrahamic covenant through whom all nations would be blessed (Gen 12:1-3). This covenant brought with it a responsibility to believe through faith in God extending to Isaac and Jacob (Hebrews 11:8-9). Abraham is the first man 'in whom the principle of justification by faith is clearly seen'[63].

e) The dispensation of Mosaic law – God provided a complete system of law for the people of Israel. Obedience to the law would bring blessing and disobedience would bring a curse. This law exposed the extent of the sinfulness of man (Galatians 3:10).

f) The dispensation of the present Church age of grace – salvation through the death of the Lord Jesus Christ brought about a new covenant bringing together all peoples, Jews and Gentiles who believe in His name. God's grace is evident throughout scripture but in the present age it becomes a ruling principle (John 1:17). Righteousness is a gift of God imputed through faith because the Lord Jesus bore the curse of the law which sets us free (Romans 8:2). The church is composed of all believers from Jewish and Gentile background, neither a continuation nor a replacement for Israel[66] but a new work.

g) The dispensation of the Kingdom – when finally, all believing people will be with the Lord forever. As the Church is removed from the earth, God will then deal with the Jewish nation. This dispensation ends with Satan being destroyed and the new eternal day with Christ beginning.

Both Ryrie[67] and Zuck[65] agree that using dispensationalism to interpret scripture requires separating Israel as a nation, and the Church as those who believe in the risen Christ. Israel and the Church are not interchangeable terms. Also as previously stated, dispensational

---

[66] Catchpole R 2021 Dispensational Theology (2) Lamp and Light The Society for Distributing Hebrew Scriptures March /April
[67] Ryrie C 1965 Dispensationalism today Moody Press

theology brings all the ages together to glorify God because this is His plan. God's dealings with mankind have differed with each dispensation[65] and yet readers of the Bible can see the same strands running through each of the ages. God is the author of all the ages and has brought about His plan of salvation with unerring grace in different ways to all mankind. So, for instance the Mosaic commandments to love your neighbour as yourself is repeated by Jesus in Matt 5:44; 19:19; 22:39 but with an understanding of why one should love one's neighbour. Yet at the same time other commandments have been swept away such as that of the law for eating unclean food (Lev 11 and Acts 10:9-16).

It is important to recognise that when interpreting scripture using dispensations students should recognise the differences between dispensations and apply them accordingly.

Causes of Disrepute

Three treatments of the method have brought dispensationalism into disrepute. The first is that it has been developed into an elaborate and inflexible doctrine[68] which contrasts with the simple approach which we are taught by the example of the author of Hebrews. Secondly, it has been the tendency to set this or that passage in a dispensation different to our own and rob it of almost all its application to us by failing to recognise the principles and doctrines which apply in every age. The third cause of damage to the image of the dispensational approach is that throughout the twentieth and twenty first centuries, some Christians have used this as the main if not exclusive way in which they interpret Scripture. In this way much of the freshness of the Word and guiding of the Holy Spirit has been lost.

The Ages in Hebrews

Although the Epistle does not contain any of the proof texts of dispensationalism, the scene is set in the opening two verses to recognise the differences of God's revelation in different ages, particularly contrasting the 'time past' when 'the fathers' were alive

---

[68] Schofield 1954 *Reference Bible and Commentary* Oxford University Press

(Heb 1:1) and 'these last days' when the Lord Jesus came as the Son revealing the Father (Heb 1:2). The incarnation of the Word is clearly seen in this passage as the watershed of the ages. Whereas no clue is given here as to the future ways in which God would govern His creation, it does look back over the Old Testament and hints at distinguishable eras. Each of these show God's distinctive way of dealing with His people or mankind in general:

In the past God spoke to our forefathers through the prophets at many times and in various ways, but in these last days he has spoken to us by his Son...' Hebrews 1:1,2

Those who use the dispensational method of understanding Scripture have developed a system of a sequence of these times with comparable structures of each and with distinctive names. But this will not fulfil the objectives of the epistle where anything more than a contrast between the dealings of God through the revelation at Sinai and the surpassing revelation through Christ, would detract from the clarity of the message of the epistle. This straightforward comparison does not entail any artificial construction of 'times/ manners' but most importantly Hebrews lays down the guidelines as to how 'dispensations' may be valuably compared. Heading's[69] book title 'Types and Shadows in the Epistle to the Hebrews' make this twofold division particularly clear. He refers to this as the tactic of the writer of the Epistle.

Other indications of the distinctions between the ages will be found in Heb 2:3: 'This salvation, which was first announced by the Lord was confirmed to us by those who heard him. God also testified...' and 9:26 '...but now he has appeared once for all at the end of the ages to do away with sin by the sacrifice of Himself.'

The passage of time and the cues for changes in God's dealings are brought out in Hebrews in the following suite of passages:

'In the beginning, O Lord, you laid the foundations of the earth, and

---

[69] Heading J 1979 *Types and Shadows in the Epistle to the Hebrews* Gospel Tract Publications Glasgow UK

the heavens are the work of your hands. They will perish, but you remain; they will all wear out like a garment. You will roll them up like a robe; like a garment they will be changed. But you remain the same, and your years will never end.' Heb 1:10-12

'A better hope is introduced, by which we draw near to God.' Heb 7:19

'The oath, which came after the law, appointed the Son, who has been made perfect for ever.' Heb 7:28

'He has made the first one obsolete; and what is obsolete and ageing will soon disappear.' Heb 8:13

'They are only a matter of food and drink and various ceremonial washings – external regulations applying until the time of the new order.' Heb 9:10

'Christ will appear a second time, not to bear sin, but to bring salvation to those who are waiting for him.' Heb 9:28

'He sets aside the first to establish the second.' Heb 10:9

'Therefore, since we are receiving a kingdom that cannot be shaken, let us be thankful, and so worship God acceptably with reverence and awe.' Heb 12:28

What a thrilling selection of verses these are! We see our God moving majestically through time with His ways suited to each age without compromise of His holiness, wisdom, and power. But notice how informally these ages are introduced by the Holy Spirit without the jerky divisions which systematic dispensationalism might lead us to expect.

The Unity of the Dispensation

There is, of course, a particular danger of emphasising the distinctions of God's dealings in different eras, and this is to entertain the idea that God changes in some way with His dispensations. 'I the Lord, do not change' He cries out in Malachi (3:6). In Hebrews too we have the antidote: 'Jesus Christ the same yesterday and today, and for ever' (13:8). We must be careful to think of the Saviour as infinitely superior to the method of dispensational interpretation. This would be especially valuable when the student is seeking caution to interpret the Lord's words in the Gospels.

We have continued to caution ourselves about compromising the immutability of God by pressing dispensational interpretation too far. It is no accident that the writer of Hebrews is led to season his contrasts between the Old and New Testaments with allusions to God's eternal character ('The Lord will not change His mind' 7:21; the immutability of His counsel 6:17; 'Your throne O God will last for ever and ever,' 1:8; 'You remain the same, and your years will never end.' 1:12; 'the eternal spirit' 9:14). Furthermore, the study of God's changing government must not detract from the immoveable kingdom (12:22) and the security of the everlasting covenant (13:20). We ought not to overemphasise the discontinuity of Scripture. After all, the introduction of Hebrews which pointed us to the different ways in which God spoke in times past, is just as much an assertion of the continuity of God's dealings: His continuous communication with our race from the beginning (Heb 1:12).

It is helpful to look at Hebrews 11 in the light of the contrasts between the ages yet at the same time recognise that they complement each other. Heb 11:2 looks back and says, 'this is what the ancients were commended for', and we note that no finer divisions are made in the chapter as to particular dispensations in which those 'ancients' exercised their faith. In fact, these all died in faith, and did not receive the promises, only seeing them from a distance (Heb 11:13). Then their relationship to we who live under the New Covenant follows (Heb 11:39,40): 'God had planned something better for us so that only together with us would they be made perfect.'

The New and Old Contrast in Hebrews

Instead of dwelling on all these different ages, the writer of Hebrews makes the core of his epistle the great contrast between the Old ready to disappear (Heb 8:13) and the New which he is emphatic is a 'better' hope 7:19; a 'better' covenant 7:22; a 'better' promise 8:6; a 'better' country 11:16; a 'better' word 12:24; and 'better' possessions 10:34. Thus we learn how to apply this dispensational method of Biblical interpretation, the comparison and contrast of the ages, which includes present and future times and God's dealings with us.

It is against this background that Hebrews sets the primary Biblical doctrine of the Supremacy of Christ. Although we turn to Hebrews most frequently to refresh our hearts with this truth, the writer wants to turn it to the practical application of giving all the saints a foundation from which absolutely nothing will tempt them to slip.

Just as surely, we must not be tempted from our standing in God's grace to any other alleged current attraction of the religious or secular world. We think especially of Christians who live in countries with invasive political ideologies, or where the fallacies of comparative religion are being promoted, or where fundamentalists of old heathen religions are on the march, or where claims of idols once worshipped are pressed upon those who 'have turned to God' (1 Thess: 1,9).

The frequency of relative and comparative words throughout Hebrews particularly suits the dispensational approach. Thus, the inadequacies of the law and the accompanying ritual are exposed especially in chapters 7 to 10. Because of its inadequacy it follows that God supersedes it by the superior and lasting New Covenant. The contrast is made point by point until little is left of present value under the Old Covenant (contrasting with Paul's treatment of the law in Romans 9-11).

We should remind ourselves that the comparisons do not stop at the supremacy of Christ, (second to none), and the superlative New Covenant He made. The responsibilities of those blessed under the New Covenant are also heavier: 'how much more severely do you think a man deserves to be punished' (Heb 10:29); 'how much less will we escape?' (12:25).

Notice the variety of words (in English) used to describe the relative inferiority of the Old Covenant: 'weak and useless (Heb 7:18); 'men who are weak' (5:2; 7:28); faulty (8:7,8); obsolete and ageing (8:13); external value only (9:10,11; 10:1); impossible to take away sin (10:4, 11).

A Dispensational view of the Old Covenant

The dispensational treatment of the Old Covenant by the author of Hebrews by no means exhausts its interpretive value for us. He shows us how to apply a typical interpretation to the same scripture but there are also spiritual lessons from the old economy for us today (in Hebrews 13:11,12 especially). Nor do these interpretations detract at all from the fact that through the Old Covenant, God's people were greatly blessed and learned His conditions for behaviour and worship. It is true that the very nature of the priestly and tabernacle ritual which should have taught them spiritual lessons became counterproductive and necessitated the prophets' correction (see Ps 51:16,17; Isa 1:10-15; Jer 7:21-24). What a wonderful Bible we have that these three different understandings are completely compatible!

Practical Exercise

1. *Take three dispensational ages and show how God gives man new responsibilities with new laws, blessings, and warnings. Then describe man's response to these responsibilities and God's judgement at the end of that age.*

2. *What is the value of using dispensational theology in interpreting the Bible?*

3. *Reading through these references again from Hebrews, how many dispensations can you identify and what relevance do they have for us today?*

'In the beginning, O Lord, you laid the foundations of the earth, and the heavens are the work of your hands. They will perish, but you remain; they will all wear out like a garment. You will roll them up like a robe; like a garment they will be changed. But you remain the same, and your years will never end.' Heb 1:10-12

'A better hope is introduced, by which we draw near to God.' Heb 7:19

'The oath, which came after the law, appointed the Son, who has been made perfect for ever.' Heb 7:28

'He has made the first one obsolete; and what is obsolete and ageing

will soon disappear.' Heb 8:13

'They are only a matter of food and drink and various ceremonial washings – external regulations applying until the time of the new order.' Heb 9:10

'Christ will appear a second time, not to bear sin, but to bring salvation to those who are waiting for him.' Heb 9:28

'He sets aside the first to establish the second.' Heb 10:9

'Therefore, since we are receiving a kingdom that cannot be shaken, let us be thankful, and so worship God acceptably with reverence and awe.' Heb 12:28

NOTES

The Case for Dispensations

CHAPTER ELEVEN
BIBLE PROPHECY

Seeing that the Bible is a book that is both human and divine, we seek to interpret it as we would any other book while at the same time affirming its uniqueness as a book of divine truth from the hand of God.

Roy Zuck

Distinguishing Fulfilled and Unfulfilled Messianic Prophecy

Following on from considering how the author of Hebrews distinguishes between God's ways of dealing with mankind in different ages, we will see how he treats prophetic scripture. Under the guidance of the Holy Spirit, he finds a Messianic key to the Old Testament. Prophecy comes from two Greek words which mean 'to speak for or before', in other words speaking or writing of events prior to their occurring[70]. So great was the author's appreciation of the greatness of Christ, that, whether or not he knew the Lord's words, he obeyed the injunction, 'You diligently study the Scriptures because you think that by them you possess eternal life. These are the Scriptures that testify about me, yet you refuse to come to me to have life' (John 5:39,40). The writer was strikingly discriminating in that he recognised the difference between fulfilled prophecy and prophecy still awaiting fulfilment, which the prophets of old were unable to distinguish (1 Peter 1:10-12, Chafer[71]).

---

[70] Zuck, R 1991 Basic Bible Interpretation: A Practical Guide to Discovering Biblical Truth Victor Publishing USA UK

[71] Chafer L 1974 Revised by Walvoord J Major Bible Themes Zondervan Press USA

Perhaps nowhere is this more obvious than his treatment of Psalm 8 in Heb 2:5-9. The dominion which man was intended to have in Gen 1:26, 28 over the creation was not assumed by Adam, but the Lord Jesus, found in fashion as a man (Phil 2:8) was recognisably worthy of this absolute dominion. Yet 'At present we do not see everything subject to Him' (Heb 2:8; Ps 110:1) so with spiritual insight he sees that the subjection of all things under His feet (Heb 2:8) is reserved for 'the world to come, about which we are speaking' (Heb 2:5).

The author sees that the words of Ps 22:22 are only truly apt when put into the Lord's mouth. 'I will declare your name to my brothers; in the presence of the congregation, I will sing your praises' (Heb 2:12) having appreciated the Lord's fulfilment of the previous 21 verses of the Psalm at Calvary. He sees a prophetic significance in the faithful service of Moses:'testifying to what would be said in the future' (Num 12:7; Heb 3:5) which leads him on to the superior position of Christ 'as a son over God's house' (Heb 3:6).

He looks at Habakkuk 2:3 and again sees that its fulfilment is still in the future, 'For just in a little while, he who is coming will come and will not delay' (Heb 10:37). What sensitive discernment was necessary to see that the Lord Jesus was specifically the subject of Habakkuk's vision. He reads Haggai 2:6,7 and interpreting the phrase 'in a little while I will once more' he sets this event at the end of time (Heb 12:25-29) contrasting it with the events at Sinai (Ex 19). This prophetic understanding of the author to Hebrews gives us a relevant challenge for today. In the light of such solid interpretation, we can be thankful that our future is in the hands of an immutable God who is giving us an 'unshakable kingdom' but is not to be trifled with for 'our God is a consuming fire' (Deut 4:24; 9:3; Heb 12:29).

Freshness of Hebrews' Prophetic Studies

It is evident that these interpretations are restrained yet daring and the signs of a mature believer feeding on the Word of God. His treatment of Ps 110:1-4 is most detailed and we will examine this more carefully in Case Study B. Most of us will feel that our guide in interpretations shows us up as being in the beginners' class.

However, Zuck[70] asserts that prophecy is not only important for our understanding of scriptures but also necessary to comfort; calm; convert; cleanse; compel and clarify both our own study of scripture but also when explaining it to others. Significantly for us today, while many biblical prophecies have been fulfilled there is still a large proportion of the Bible which has not yet been accomplished. The Bible student cannot therefore afford to ignore eschatological interpretation when reading the Bible as a whole. Every single word spoken by the Creator God holds significance for the passage of time from Genesis to Revelation, which is the timeline of our whole world. Therefore, it is important to note that the interpretation of prophecy should be carried out in the same way that the rest of the Bible is interpreted. Where there are literal statements such as that seen in Isaiah 65:20, they should be seen as actually happening in the future. Where the figurative use of language is employed then the scenes described will be either symbolic (Rev 13:1-4) or so outside of the prophet's worldview (Rev 9:7-10) that he can only use the words he has in his world view dictionary.

The Bible student therefore has two main objectives when interpreting prophecy:

1. To distinguish between those prophecies that have been fulfilled and those which are yet to come.

2. To ensure that all interpretation points towards the coming Messiah and His future reign in the new heaven and the new earth.

Before we leave this brief account of the use of the prophetic scriptures in Hebrews, we note Westcott's[72] observation that 'no direct prophetic word is quoted.' The writer of Hebrews is seeking to break new ground in Old Testament exposition. As Westcott[72] puts it, to the writer, it is that the Old Testament does not simply contain prophecies but that it is one vast prophecy.

---

[72] Westcott B 2nd Ed 1892 The Epistle to the Hebrews: The Greek text with notes and essays Macmillan and Co Scotland

Practical Exercise

1. *Examine the passage in Hebrews 12:25-29, comparing it with Exodus 19 and Revelation 20:11-15. Describe the reason for reverence and awe which must accompany God who is holy above all others.*

2. *In what ways would Hebrews 13:14 be able to comfort; calm; convert; cleanse, and compel listeners when attempting to clarify world events in the light of the words 'here we do not have an enduring city'?*

3. *On the Day of Pentecost, a small portion of Joel 2 was fulfilled. As you read this chapter reflect on where the rest of the fulfilment of this prophecy fits in the Bible as a whole.*

NOTES

Chapter Twelve
Bible Topics

Even a casual reader of the Bible soon discovers he is reading a most unusual book.

Lewis Chafer

The topical approach to the interpretation of scripture is especially important in seeking a balanced and biblical view of a subject. It entails, first of all, choosing a topic which is of particular significance in the interpreter's own spiritual experience or that of those to whom the Word of God is being ministered. It might be a subject of contention, or which has been neglected, misunderstood or of special profit in current circumstances. The choice of this topic is of utmost spiritual significance, requiring earnest prayer. By using the available aids to Bible Study (particularly concordances and marginal cross-references) the student gathers as many of the scriptural allusions to the topic as feasible. Careful reading and comparison of these leads to a balanced appreciation of the scope of the subject and provides illustrations of its operation in the context of biblical history.

A Topical Subject in Hebrews

Once again, the writer of Hebrews provides us with perhaps the clearest example of the use of the topical method in the New Testament and calls on the Old Testament as his source to explore the breadth of his subject. I am referring, of course, to the topic of faith to which Hebrews 11 is devoted; called memorably by Sauer[73] 'The arena of faith.' The writer of the epistle chose this topic because it is central to his theme of encouraging believers to remain firm in faithfulness to the Lord and not to be distracted or attracted by any unsubstantiated alternative. So, we must see the chapter of faith in the context of such passages as 'holding on to our courage and the hope of which we boast '(Heb 3:6) compared with 'see to it, brothers, that none of you has a sinful, unbelieving heart that turns away from the living God' (3:12) and also 'if we hold firmly till the end the confidence we had at first' (3:14); 'no-one falls by following their example of disobedience' (4:11); full assurance of faith (10:22) and profession of faith (10:23); 'Jesus, the author and perfecter of our faith' (12:2).

The key verse which he wants to illustrate is the principle of faith in Hab 2:4: 'Now my righteous one will live by faith. And if he shrinks back, I will not be pleased with him' (Heb 10:38) and therefore, 'without faith it is impossible to please God' (Heb 11:6). In his search of Old Testament men and women of faith the writer finds how extensive is his topic and how many-faceted. Out of the 23 Old Testament characters to whom he refers in the letter, 19 of these are mentioned in this chapter. He sees the operation of the principle of faith in personal and national history. He discovers that this spiritual quality is often exhibited in the mundane things of life (Heb 11:10, 15, 26 and 13:14). The significance of the acts of faith was that they were the first to apply the principle in the circumstances so that their implicit trust in God's power was without precedence which went on to provide an example for many later generations. Nor was the author's simply a mechanical concordance or study for the actual word 'faith' came into rather few of his stories. Once again, his intimate knowledge of the Old Testament was used by the Holy Spirit. Each story had to be scrutinized to see what was produced by faith. We remind ourselves that this was not an exhaustive treatment of the exercise of faith in the Old Testament. The student could do worse than complete it himself: 'what more shall I say? I do not have time to tell about Gideon and Barak' (Heb 11:32).

---

[73] Sauer E 1955 The Arena of Faith Paternoster Press UK

Other Topics in Hebrews

The other example of topical studies from the Old Testament in the epistle to the Hebrews, are not as full as the study on faith. In fact, these are doctrines which the Old Testament Scriptures are called upon for support. One of these is the place of covenants in God's dealings with His people. Although we will look more carefully later at the writer's interpretation of Jeremiah 31:31-34, we will notice that he is comparing this (Heb 8:8-12) with the covenant which Moses was instrumental in bringing to Israel. The superiority of the Lord Jesus in bringing in a new covenant (Heb 10:5) and the ways in which it is better (Heb 8:6; 10:29; 13:20) challenge those involved in it to live consistently with its basis. There is a close link with the dispensational approach, reflected in the Old and New Testaments and referring to the Hebrew and Christian scriptures. Ryrie[74] tries to draw a sharp distinction between Covenant theology and Dispensational theology, yet it is clearly of value to recognise the way in which in each dispensation God gives men grounds for committing themselves to His faithfulness.

The writer of Hebrews also studied the topic of the priesthood which derived from Aaron. He looked at the duties, office, service, fasting, succession, and maintenance, of these priests. And from this topical study he saw the ways in which the Lord Jesus outshone each and every one of them, earning the new title 'Great High Priest' (Heb 4:14). This, of course, borders on the typological method of interpretation examined in Chapter 15, but we note it here because of this godly man's extensive study of his subject in the Old Testament. Familiarity with the topic was a pre-requisite of his interpretation.

Authors who have written on the book of Hebrews contend that the topics the author chose was for specific reasons. Morris[75] goes along with the traditional view that the recipients were Jewish Christians tempted to relapse into Judaism. Wright[76] holds this view but broadens

---

[74] Ryrie C 1965 Dispensationalism today Moody Press

[75] Morris L 1978 Understanding the New Testament Published by Holman UK

[76] Wright T 2003 *Hebrews for Everyone* Published by Society for Promoting Christian Knowledge UK

it out to give a gracious understanding of the cultural worldview of Jewish Christians at the time. His discussion focuses on the fact that Hebrews is an 'argument designed to show you cannot go back to an earlier stage of God's purpose but must go forwards'.

Whatever the purpose of Hebrews, the author has given us a wide range of topics that he has circumnavigated in his desire to fix our eyes upon Jesus who is central to our faith. These topics include:

- The Revelation of God Hebrews 1:1-4
- The superiority of Christ to angels 1:5-14
- This great salvation 2:1-4
- Jesus crowned 2:5-9
- The manhood, yet deity of Christ 2:10-18
- The superiority of Christ to Moses and therefore the law 3:1-6
- Disobedience 3:7-11
- An evil and unbelieving heart 3:12-19
- God's Rest 4:1-13
- Christ our great High Priest 4:14 – 5:11
- Spiritual Immaturity 5:12-6:3
- Apostasy 6:4-8; 10:26-31
- Encouragement to persevere 6:9-12; 10:32-39
- Immutability of God's promises 6:13-20
- Melchizedek' priesthood 7:1-14
- A better hope 7:15-19
- A better covenant 7:20-25
- The perfect Son 7:26-28
- The reality of what is to come 8:1-7
- The new covenant compared to the old covenant 8:8-13
- The tabernacle for today 9:1-10
- Christ's sacrifice 9:11-28; 10:11-18; 13:7-16
- The will of God 10:1-10
- The response of a Christlike heart 10:19-25
- Faith 11:1-40
- Christ our example 12:1-3
- Discipline 12:4-10
- Suffering 12:11-17
- The City of God and His holiness 12:18-29
- Christian Service 13:1-6, 17-25

Bible Topics

Thirty significant topics found in one sermon is no mean feat! Hence the reason for a certain reluctance on the part of Bible students to investigate Hebrews with an enquiring mind. However, Hebrews is a springboard to the whole of the rest of the Bible and as we have seen in previous chapters the positive outcomes from such study are both life-changing and of lasting value.

Practical Exercise

1. *The Hebrews author finishes his sermon with two extremely contentious topics – sex and money. Read the final chapter of Hebrews in the light of his whole discourse and discuss his reasoning for:*

   a) *Juxtaposing the two subjects of sex and money*

   b) *Why he put these subjects at the end of his sermon, leaving his listeners with a mega challenge in the briefest of explanations.*

2. *Take one topic from the Hebrews list of thirty topics above and examine it in the light of the rest of scripture, noting all references to this subject.*

3. *What is the biblical topic that is on your heart right now? Does the book of Hebrews speak into this topic? If not, where can you go in the Bible to find a Godly exposition of this topic?*

NOTES

God Speaks

CHAPTER THIRTEEN
BIBLICAL BIOGRAPHY

Faith is being sure of what we hope for and certain of what we do not see. This is what the ancients were commended for

Hebrews 11:1,2

Intimate Knowledge of Old Testament Personalities

There is a significance in the number of times people are mentioned in the Bible and who mentions them. For instance, when Jesus speaks of prophets of old, he is talking of his foretelling and their specific contribution to God's plan of salvation (Noah: Matt 24:37 and Jonah: Matt 12:39). In Hebrews we find many significant people, and a further explanation of the number of times they are mentioned is given in Appendix 1.

The writer's exemplary familiarity with the Old Testament Scriptures is nowhere better illustrated than by his knowledge of the men and women of the Bible. A superficial reading of Hebrews will impress us with the references he makes to twenty-three characters in all. Moses appears nine times (and only six of the chapters fail to mention him); Abraham and Melchizedek eight times. Only the last chapter names no-one from the Old Testament (but Timothy is there!). Of course, in his study of faith, the writer mentions ten of the names just once.

---

[77] McKeen J 2020 *The Model Sermon: Principles of Preaching from the Book of Hebrews* Published by Christianity Today

McKeen[77] states that the author of Hebrews used character studies to illustrate principles of Christian living. For instance, Noah and Abraham remained courageous in the face of enormous obstacles (11:7,11) but were both given promises by God which they held onto throughout their eventful lives. These promises resulted in global consequences then and now, ultimately fulfilled in the future. This helps to emphasise that the Bible contains the history of many individuals and the use of their names is a pointer to their individuality and accountability to God.

Hebrews on Melchizedek

The detail given in scripture about any one of the Bible personalities can often be interpreted in terms of examples to follow or avoid. In some instances, certain features of their biographies will be reminiscent of others, or more importantly of Christlike characteristics. The writer of Hebrews shows how much may be gained from looking at quite a minor Old Testament character called Melchizedek. Although we will look at the story in detail later (Case Study B), it is sufficient here to notice that he makes use of the translation of the man's name and of the place where he lived (Heb 7:2). Many editions of the Bible give translations in the margin and provide valuable aids to interpretation, often being suited to the character of the person or place. Undoubtedly authors were led by the Holy Spirit to give these names. This is a special case of verbal inspiration (see Chapter 8). Once again it is possible to become a slave to this method and fanciful connections can be made between the name and the career. It may be that the meanings of some of the names are not at all certain given the time and culture difference between then and now. This emphasises the need to be under the discipline of the Spirit when handling Scripture, as were its writers.

Moses in Egypt, and Abel

We readily appreciate the writer's interpretation of the story of Moses in Egypt (Heb 11:23-27) as he shows that faith governed his actions and those of his parents. See how he applies the experience to the believer following the Saviour (13:13) and the choice which we face confronted by affliction or the pleasures of sin for the gospel testimony today. Again, watch how he brings alive the few verses about Abel (Gen 4:2-10; Heb 11:4; 12:24): the speaking blood of a murdered godly man.

It is only when we start to really dip into these biographies that we see just how closely the Hebrews author has examined their lives and found godly treasure of eternal value. All of these people lived normal lives with challenges, joy, and pain, disobeying God often yet trying to serve Him within their human capacity. God amply rewarded them by commending them for their faith even although none of them received what they had been promised (Heb 11:39). That reward is still to come when all believers will receive their reward from the King together and become perfect together in so doing (Heb 11:40).

Practical Exercise

1. *Choose a character from Hebrews 11 and write a biographical account of their life, including the direction of their faith pointing to Jesus.*

2. *Reflect on those people who lives have had a significant impact on your own Christian faith. What was it about their lives that made you want to emulate them and how did you put that into effect in your life?*

3. *Take time to watch this biographical video on the life of Charles Spurgeon, a young teenager who sought the Lord and found him: https://www.youtube.com/watch?v=cKYQW5KB40U*

NOTES

God Speaks

Chapter Fourteen
Interpreting Hebrew Ritual

'To the weak I become weak, to win the weak. I have become all things to all men so that by all possible means I might save some. I do all this for the sake of the gospel, that I may share in its blessings.'

1 Corinthians 9:22,23

In chapters 4-10, 12 and 13 of Hebrews the author of the epistle makes considerable but balanced use of the ceremony which God commanded Israel to observe on the way to Canaan across the wilderness. He neither treats this as an irrelevant and unintelligible ritual of an earlier age which some seem to do today, nor at the other extreme, an illustration of every New Testament thought. Instead he declares that the student needs to learn to focus on the chosen subject rather than chase unneeded detail (Heb 9:5).

What encouraged the writer so much to make use of these Old Testament ceremonies was his discovery that they were not intended merely to serve a dispensation, but they were copied from enduring patterns (Heb 8:2,5; 9:24; Ex 25:9) which clearly do and will serve purposes in heaven. What these purposes are may not yet be clear to us (although Rev 3:12; 8:3,4; 11:19 gives some indication), but it is sufficient to know that Moses was not copying trivial or transient things. The caution with which Moses copied the tabernacle and its furniture serves as a warning to us to make full and careful use of information he has left us, to interpret it reverently and relevantly to our day. The uses to which these articles and the way people were employed about them both for sacrifices, feasts and priestly duties

God Speaks

are of great interpretable value.

The writer recognised that the Holy Spirit himself invested these things (and those whose task it was to use them) with significance far beyond their value to Israel (Heb 9:8). How then can a Christian ignore his responsibility to search out their value?

To give an idea of the extensive use of the tabernacle and its accoutrements in Hebrews, it is helpful to articulate this in a visual form as seen in Table 3:

Table 3: Items of worship from the Old Testament tabernacle in Hebrews. Brackets denote 'alluding to' description

Item of worship	Reference
The Sanctuary or tabernacle	Hebrews 8:2; 8:5; 9:1; 9:2; 9:8; 13:10; 9:11,21,24
Gifts and sacrifices	Hebrews [1:3;] 5:1,3; 7:27; 8:3,4; 9:[7],9; 9:[12-14],23,28; 10:1,3, 5,6,8,11-14,18,26; 11:17; [13:12], 15,16,[20]
The Most Holy Place or inner sanctuary	Hebrews 6:19,20; 9:3,8,12,25;10:19; 13:11
Tithing	Hebrews 7:5-10
The lampstand	Hebrews 9:2
The table	Hebrews 9:2
The consecrated bread	Hebrews 9:2; [13:9]
The Holy Place	Hebrews 9:2
The Golden Altar of Incense	Hebrews 9:4
Ark of the Covenant	Hebrews 9:4
Gold Jar of Manna	Hebrews 9:4
Aaron's staff that budded	Hebrews 9:4
The Stone Tablets of the covenant	Hebrews 9:4
The Cherubim of the Glory	Hebrews 9:5
Ceremonial washing	Hebrews 9:10, 19; [10:22;] 11:28; 12:24

134

Water, scarlet wool, branches of hyssop	Hebrews 9:19
The Curtain	Hebrews 10:20
The Altar	Hebrews 13:10
Priestly ministers	Hebrews 2:17; 4:14,15; 5:1-6; 6:20; 7:1,3,5,11-17,20,21,23-28; 8:1-4; 9:6,7; 9:11; 10:11,12; 13:11
Day of Atonement	Hebrews 2:17; 9:7,12,25,28; 10:1; 12:24

When there appear to be descriptive lists in scripture it is helpful to log this in a visual way so that the student can compare and contrast at a glance without having to keep returning to commentaries and memory.

The Hebrews author uses different techniques to draw lessons from these lists but clearly, the Bible student cannot afford to neglect the study of Exodus, Leviticus, Numbers and Deuteronomy. Whichever church first received the epistle, they were expected to understand all the allusions to the Levitical ceremony associated with the first covenant, and, certainly, Gentile believers should come to it with no less a working knowledge.

Alongside an understanding of the Old Testament tabernacle rituals, it is also important to recognise the cultural differences between social groups not only in terms of nationality – but also in different eras. The first century nomadic tribes of Africa differ enormously to the twenty-first century growing cities of the African continent. Language, dress, customs, rituals, and food all play a part in an individual's world view. For instance, Zuck[78] points out that when the Jews returned from their exile in Babylon, they probably returned speaking Aramaic, hence the reason for the Levites having to translate the law for the people (Neh 8:8). It is important therefore, when interpreting scripture, to take

---

[78] Zuck, R 1991 *Basic Bible Interpretation: A Practical Guide to Discovering Biblical Truth* Victor Publishing USA UK

cognisance of cultural influences which include evolving changes in language, dress, and customs over a period of time.

Practical Exercise

1. *Hebrews 13 cites various rituals that are now obsolete (13:9-11), but discusses other cultural values (13:2-5, 16-17) which carry the same principles today.*

   a) *Discuss why those rituals are obsolete and what has replaced them.*

   b) *List the cultural values found in these verses and apply them to four countries around the world, noting the differences.*

   c) *If you were to take the gospel to each of these four countries, what applications could you make of the differences in cultures that you have learned?*

2. *Trace the building of the tabernacle from Exodus, through Hebrews, to its eventual unveiling before God's people in Revelation. What differences are there between the 'prototype' in Exodus and the reality in heaven? What relevance does this have for us today?*

3. *Hebrews 9:8 holds a significance for both believers and unbelievers today. Describe the implications of entering the Most Holy Place for both these groups of people.*

NOTES

CHAPTER FIFTEEN
WHAT IS TYPOLOGY?

'Typology enables us to see God's design of history, as He chose certain persons, events, and things in Israel to depict and predict aspects of Christ and His relationship to believers today.'

Roy Zuck

As far back as Irenaeus (130-202 AD), biblical scholars have been using typology to interpret the New Testament in the light of the Old Testament. While Irenaeus' typology may have sometimes been extreme[79] he was severe in criticising other theologians for taking Bible passages out of context or interpreting in the light of their own theories. We need to be unendingly tied to the specifics of Scripture, says Traub[80] using Scripture to interpret Scripture rather than being taken prisoner by allegorizing or overusing typology. If, when using typology or any other method, you find yourself missing out on the person of Christ, then you are in danger of focusing on yourself and your method rather than on Jesus. Traub[80] asserts that the New Testament is the official interpreter of the Old, but the Old Testament lays a foundation for the New and we cannot understand the one without the other.

---

[79] Zuck, R 1991 *Basic Bible Interpretation: A Practical Guide to Discovering Biblical Truth* Victor Publishing USA UK

[80] Traub W 2021 'How to interpret and apply the OT today' Lecture 6 on Hebrews Edinburgh Theological Seminary

It is important to distinguish between allegory and typology, for as Zuck[79] says, typology easily slips into allegorizing. Allegory says that the literal meaning of the text does not matter for it is the hidden meaning that is important, while typology asserts that it is the picture of Christ found in the text which holds the greater meaning[80].

A 'type' says Wright[81] is 'the representation of a permanent and a greater truth by a thing or an event which also has a real existence and a significance of its own.' Zuck[79] pares this back to the Greek word *typos* used in the New Testament in a variety of ways: mark (John 20:25); form (Rom 6:17); pattern (Heb 8:5); model (1 Thess 1:7); example (Titus 2:7). All of these match or resemble one another[79].

McKeen[82] is quick to point out that Hebrews demonstrates from the whole Bible how the Old Testament characters tell the story of the real story – that is our Lord Jesus Christ. They were in fact the shadow of the things to come (Heb 10:1; Col 2:17). The reading of any story – historical, poetic, prophecy or law – all point to the main character of the Bible, the one whom the Word of God is introducing to the world.

It may be very glib to say that typology is a 'type' of this or that, but what exactly does the interpreter mean when he is required to be justified in his interpretation? Encouraging the use of typology when commenting on Hebrews 5, Gooding[83] writes 'that to reject typology is not always a sign of good theology, it can be an indication of spiritual babyhood.' Berkhof[84] devotes some space to defining 'types plus their helpful warnings or their misuse'. Heading's[85] book despite its title, compounds the difficulties in calling the treatment of Melchizedek (Heb 7:1-3) an allegory, noting the example and

---

[81] Wright J S 1955 *Interpreting the Bible* Intervarsity Fellowship UK

[82] McKeen J 2020 T*he Model Sermon: Principles of Preaching from the Book of Hebrews* Published by Christianity Today

[83] Gooding D 1976 *An Unshakeable Kingdom Ten Studies on the Epistle to the Hebrews* Everyday Publications Canada

[84] Berkhof L 1950 Principles of Biblical Interpretation (sacred hermeneutics) Baker Bookhouse Grand Rapids, Michigan USA

[85] Heading J 1979 *Types and Shadows in the Epistle to the Hebrews* Gospel Tract Publications Glasgow UK

shadow (Heb 7:3) and later recognising much typological material in the epistle, but not really explaining how to interpret types. However, Zuck[79] helpfully gives five elements necessary when defining an official type: resemblance; historical reality; prefiguring (predictive or foreshadowing element); heightening (where the antitype is superior to the type); and divine design. Later he adds a sixth element which is that it must be designated in the New Testament. The epistle to the Hebrews helps us overcome the problems of types.

Types in Hebrews and their allies

The author starts off from the literal Old Testament narrative, the historical record or ritual. At the same time, the writer wants us to realise that the Old Testament feature is intentionally reported to be a help to us in our study of eternal truths by the aid of the Holy Spirit. There is no question of suggesting that the stories were metaphorical or allegorical, the interpretation goes beyond this by making the comparison between the Old Testament and a New Testament doctrine or person. The latter is to be considered vastly more significant than the former and the Epistle introduces us to works which show how insubstantial the Old Testament feature is compared to its New Testament counterpart.

In Heb 4:11 (3:17) he has spoken of the Israelites who died in the wilderness on their way to Canaan. These he said were an 'example' of disobedience. The Greek word suggests that something is being held up for our consideration either to follow, teach or warn us. It may even suggest that the lesson needs discernment although of all the words used, it is applied to the most obvious lesson drawn from the Old Testament. The translation of the same word in Hebrews 9:23 is more difficult. The realities (or copies, NIV) in the heavens (things requiring sanctification which only Christ could accomplish) cannot be 'patterns' ('similarities' might be the best word), bringing out the comparison for us to think about. Perhaps Hebrews 8:5 helps us here because we are told that the place of service of the Old Testament priests was an example (the same word again) or a shadow of what is in heaven. A shadow (as in Heb 10:1 where the same is foreshadowing of Col 2:17) tells us that although it is flat and insubstantial, reality is nearby; it requires that light shines upon a concrete object to produce the shadow. The tabernacle was in the shade of a far more worthy heavenly pattern. Interpretation of the Old Testament as shadows is less positive than examples or types (a word which harks back to the impression made by a blow such as a typewriter). Although there is contention over the translation of Hebrews 9:9, the tabernacle there is called a parable (or figure) by the Holy Spirit who has brought together the old to illuminate the less tangible new. Parables are extended comparisons (Heb 11:19) or, as here, contrasts.

Picture taken by ERCR of the Tabernacle display by Phil Widdison Counties Evangelist UK 1970

Matthew 13:10-23; 36-43 can be used to learn how parables are interpreted. If the tabernacle and its furniture were representative of the realities in heaven (Heb 9:23) then the writer of Hebrews introduces us to another significant word in this study which is 'figures'. Moses faithfully made copies of the real things in heaven and these copies are 'figures' (AV Heb 9:24; 'copies' NIV), antitypes which is the same suggestion as the relation of a mould to a cast.

This word *antitypos* in Greek is used twice in the New Testament according to Zuck[86]. In 1 Pet 3:21 it speaks of water baptism as an antitype of the Great Flood. The flood was for the wicked, but the waters of baptism identified the believer with Christ. In Heb 9:24, where the holy place of the tabernacle was a pattern of the true tabernacle in heaven showing that 'the antitype is greater than and superior to the type'[86].

Whilst the situation is rather confused by some Greek words being translated into various English words and some Greek words being translated into the same English word, the careful student will begin to see that one Old Testament illustration of New Testament truth cannot be labelled a type, another a shadow, yet another a parable and a fourth an example. Rather, all these suggestive words may be applied to the same Old Testament picture and our interpretation will consider all the rich ways of approaching the enduring antitype which is the blessed enjoyment or hope of the present-day believer.

The Holy Spirit's Object in employing Types

We therefore do not need to think of typology as some relatively recent and fanciful mode of interpretation of scripture. Rather, it is the Holy Spirit's way of 'signifying' (Heb 9:8) by way of comparison, or even contrast, using records which He in the first place inspired, to explain eternal subjects which we might otherwise fail to grasp. Because of the wonder and greatness of the Person of Christ we are bound to fail to appreciate Him as we ought. Since it is the task of the Spirit to reveal the Lord Jesus to His people (John 16:13-15), appreciation of the ways He uses Scripture to achieve this end is of the greatest importance.

It is therefore not surprising that some of the most rewarding typological studies will have the Lord as the Great Antitype. In

---

[86] Zuck, R 1991 *Basic Bible Interpretation: A Practical Guide to Discovering Biblical Truth* Victor Publishing USA UK

[87] Wright J S 1955 *Interpreting the Bible* Intervarsity Fellowship UK

other words, says Wright[87] the Jewish ritual law no longer has any significance, for its meaning has been completely fulfilled in Christ Himself. The law once pointed to God, and if kept, gave access to God. But this could never be the complete story, for sinful man could not possibly keep the law, despite God's mercy and grace. The whole of the Old Testament proved that it was an impossible task. So, Christ came and through His death and sacrifice of a perfect life, our sins could be forgiven forever – if we repent. This annulled the law after Christ, but it did not dismiss the significance of the law before Christ, rather it became a type which pointed to Christ.

Wright[87] uses the symbolism of money to make his point, and this can be brought up to date with present currency. Paper money and coins are becoming less used in our twenty-first century world. Smart phones, pay-cards and 'tapping' for the bill reduces our contact with 'real' money every day. But that does not make the previous money worthless. We have many possessions to show for our purchases in the pre digital days: homes, cars, furniture, holidays... Money in the past, valid for a time, has been replaced by a new monetary system which will itself one day be replaced. It is the same with the types of the Old Testament – useful and valid for a time but now replaced by Christ Himself, come to eternally replace all that was in the past.

Symbols

A symbol has meaning or significance in what it portrays[88], particularly a material object representing something abstract. It is representative of something else without any time reference, whereas a type is fulfilled at a specific time[86]. This is mostly found amongst the books of the prophets where they are often given objects to describe the situation that Israel found itself in. For instance, Jeremiah was told to go and watch the potter at work (Jeremiah 18:2) and then later to buy a clay jar which he broke in front of the elders and priests of the people. This foretold the disaster which was about to fall on all the Jews because of their disobedience to God. It would be far too easy to

[88] Reynolds E Davis M 1988 *Types, Patterns and Shadows* Precious Seed November/December Vol 39 No.6

make much of the clay pot (as in who or what it might represent) and its significance but in fact it is merely a clay pot symbolising the truth of God's punishment which was to 'smash this nation and this city just as this potter's jar is smashed and cannot be repaired (Jeremiah 19:11).'

There are three basic rules in symbolic interpretation[86]: the object itself; what the symbol refers to and the meaning. The prophet Ezekiel was given symbols throughout his period of prophesying to try and draw the people of Israel's attention to the consequences of their disobedience: the eating of a scroll (Ezek 3:3); lying on his left side for 390 days and cooking bread over cow dung (Ezek 4); packing a bag to leave (Ezek 12:4); even the death of his wife was used as symbolism (Ezek 24:16).

Various symbols in the Bible are used regularly to depict a person, object, or situation. For instance, a shepherd, lamb, or lion is used to depict Christ depending on the point of reference. When determining the meaning of symbols, ensure that you assign the symbol to its normal use and check the use of scripture for this symbol elsewhere.

There are other symbols used in scripture, for instance numbers. The numbers 7 and 40 have particular significance. Seven denotes perfection in the Garden of Eden (Gen 2:2-3) and is continued throughout Scripture as an ideal for various situations in society. Forty symbolises a time of testing or temptation: Jesus was tempted for 40 days in the wilderness (Luke 4:2), Israel was given 40 years in the desert (Num 32:13). Temptation has an ending: it does not go on forever.

Names in Scripture also carry symbolic significance, although it would be easy to take this too far. But some are obvious: Eve as the mother of all living (Gen 3:20); Peter as the rock (John 1:42). Symbolic colours are also used in the Bible but a similar warning is attached to this as with numbers and names. Zuck[86] reminds us to avoid reading into Scripture something that is not there.

An Allegory

Wright[87] defines an allegory as 'the depiction of a truth by a story that can be enjoyed as a story though the events did not, and often could not, occur in the form in which they are stated.' There are two classic allegories in literature that fit this description. John Bunyan's *Pilgrims Progress*, and C.S. Lewis' cosmic trilogy or indeed his Narnian series. Both these authors used allegory widely to enable readers to enjoy a story but to strike a much deeper note that would cause them to reflect on and perhaps turn from their present fallen state in the world.

As Wright[87] points out, we must be cautious with allegorical interpretation, as it can easily make a Bible passage less challenging and can make the Bible fit in with current thought. He cites the story of the Garden of Eden where some would interpret this as an allegory rather than a literal account of the fall of man, and thus ignore the detailed factual and geographical references in Genesis 2:10-14. As pointed out previously in the difference between typology and allegory, there is a danger of adhering to the deeper meaning of the text without pointing to Christ.

We may note in passing that the writer of Hebrews does himself write an allegory in Hebrews 6:7-8, reusing allegories in Psalm 65:10 and Isa 5:6. The student may profitably contrast this with the typology which is such a basic method freely used in the epistle.

The concluding paragraph of Reynolds[88] and Davis' article, of which the full text is to be found in Appendix 2, draws some general lessons from studies of the words used to describe the great Old Testament illustrations of New Testament doctrine. Various words used to describe figures and types in scripture are virtually interchangeable. Types are used, namely, to show that God, who is in complete control of history, has always been working progressively through human history towards the full revelation of Himself and His plan of salvation in Christ. An earlier aspect of His revelation can throw light on His later full revelation, and His full revelation can explain all aspects of His earlier revelation. This is the basic theology of typology.

Practical Exercise

1. *Explore the terms 'copy', 'shadow', 'true', 'heavenly things' and 'good things' in relation to the Book of Hebrews. How relevant are these terms to Christians in the twenty-first century?*

2. *What was the relevance of Melchizedek as a type of Christ to the Hebrew author and the point that he was making in his sermon?*

3. *Take time out to read Chapter Eight of Zuck's book Basic Bible Interpretation and test your knowledge on page 183 which gives a list of 37 illustrations of types and allegories.*

NOTES

What is Typology?

CHAPTER SIXTEEN
AN ANTIDOTE TO CARNAL RELIGION

'God envisaged from the beginning the way in which the wickedness and frailty of His human creatures would be dealt with so that the entire world...could be put into proper order'

Tom Wright

Danger of Emphasising Ritual

There is an inherent danger in making considerable use of the Old Testament: a danger of which the writer of the epistle was perfectly aware. This danger is that the interpreter might be thought to be promulgating the practices of the past dispensation. Someone might imagine that if we speak of the altar, the lampstand, the priesthood, and the sacrifices of the tabernacle, we are promoting or condoning ritualistic religion and a priestly class in the church today. As the people listened to (or read) the Hebrews sermon, they may have been thinking that if the author was using such types to illustrate even greater truths, why could they not copy those things in their day? Indeed, those who practice rituals in ornate 'places of worship' will tell us that they help ordinary people to grasp the truths of Christianity. These are also illustrations to be interpreted, they assert.

As the temple was almost certainly still in existence and being used when Hebrews was written, was there not even more danger of drawing attention to the Old Testament ways? Notice, however, that the writer avoids speaking of the temple and only refers to the tabernacle.

Wright[89] uses the illustration of an unfinished road with temporary roadways which should not be mistaken for the real thing. While the road user might get used to the chaos and confusion of a transitory highway for the perhaps long duration of building, they should still be longing for the finished article. Similarly, believers in the Lord Jesus should not be content with the past which was a transitory journey through the desert. All the effects used on that journey within the tabernacle were merely momentary, to be used temporarily until the final answer to mankind's sin was put in place through the death of Jesus Christ.

No matter how well we know the Old Testament, it is only a shadow of what we know now and so all our thoughts and energies in studying, while recognizing the importance of the past as a foundation, should be channelled onto the person and work of Christ.

Spiritual to be preferred

It is so easy to be carried away by the joy of learning, especially when it comes to the Bible and the truths that are inherent in our lives which resonate with our souls. Let us remind ourselves how the Lord, when speaking to His disciples about His flesh and His blood, lest He should cause His listeners to stumble said: 'The Spirit gives life; the flesh counts for nothing: the words that I have spoken to you are spirit, and they are life.' (John 6:63). He was reminding them that the meaning of His words was spiritual, not literal and physical.

Even parables can be dangerous to the unwary. John Bunyan thought his allegory *'Pilgrim's Progress'* was so facile that he took care to warn his readers not to be misled by the story. He wanted them to realise that it was an allegory of spiritual truths.

Since the theme of Hebrews is that the Christian has so great a salvation and an incomparable Saviour, any falling away in any direction is not to be contemplated. This seems the basis of the writer's caution in Chapter 13 rather than that he felt they were

---

[89] Wright T 2003 *Hebrews for Everyone* Published by Society for Promoting Christian Knowledge UK

particularly prone to turn to temple worship. The core message of this chapter is a confidence in the One who is our only helper and who will never change. Consequently, our hearts are raised to Him in deep thankfulness and worship for suffering alone and in disgrace for what we ourselves deserve. Our worship should be from our hearts as God desires 'in spirit and in truth (John 4:24). Indeed, it is not only in the New Testament that God's requirement for spiritual worship is set out. It is present in the Old Testament too:

- Psalm 40:6-8: The analogy of a slave shows the depth of commitment required for worshipping God. We have nothing to give to God but our hearts.
- Hebrews 10:5-8: The ultimate worship of Christ was to offer Himself to God.
- 1 Samuel 15:22-23: The danger of sacrifice is that it can become an external platitude which God sees right through.
- Psalms 50:7-15: God desires internal righteousness not external rituals.
- Hebrews 13:15: Our worship of God springs from a continual recognition of what Jesus has done for us.
- Proverbs 21:3: Worship generates right and just practices.
- Ps 51:16-17: We can truly worship from our hearts when we know the depths from which we have been saved.
- Isa 1:10-15: True worship of the living God must have a response from the worshipper that is spiritual and scriptural.
- Jer 7:21-24: Obedience is the key to worship from the heart.

The writer of Hebrews understood this key to true worship and wanted his listeners to move away from the external practices of the law which could no longer save their souls. His ability to articulate this lay in his personal passion for what Christ had done for him. Whenever we want to pass on our knowledge of what we have learned in scripture, it must always be with the same passion that this writer had, otherwise it becomes a dry academic exercise.

There are three uses of the Levitical instructions of the Old Testament, and these are not incompatible with one another. In the first place it had its literal and practical place in God's economy for His people after he had brought them out of Egypt's slavery. By this they were taught

God's standards of Holiness and His requirements when standards were broken. Secondly there is the Christological interpretation of standards showing that all the shortcomings of the approach to God through the tabernacle, its priests and service, have been adequately filled by the Saviour. But in Hebrews 13:9-16, the Old Testament regime is interpreted in a third way, drawing from it spiritual lessons relevant to the believer today. Whereas chapters 1 to 10 are a typical approach to the Old Testament, Chapter 13 is rather more parabolic. Just as a parabolic mirror behind a spotlight projects a parallel beam so Christ is given the centre stage, offering an age of grace and no longer the external rituals that could not bring lasting peace. The author brings out a spiritual interpretation which should dissuade any believer from copying Old Testament ritual. Now he is no longer writing of the Lord's fulfilment of the Old Testament but of the believers' worship superseding tabernacle worship.

In Hebrews 9:10 we read of the external value of tabernacle food and ceremonial washing rites. But the next verses turn our attention to the Christ, who did not go through the elaborate rituals established way back in the desert. Instead, the perfect man who was God entered the place of the cross and as a perfect sacrifice was able to 'cleanse our consciences from acts that lead to death' (Heb 9:14). So here in Heb 13:9 the author states categorically that it is 'not with ceremonial foods' but rather the believer's heart 'established with grace' that offers the real sacrifice God has been asking for all the way down through the ages. Whereas in 9:10 the food came from the altar, our spiritual food excludes attention to physical altars. As Wright[90] pithily puts it 'you need grace in the heart, not a special kind of food in the stomach!' If Hebrews 9:10 speaks of 'washings' to cleanse and sanctify, in 13:12 our sanctification is associated with Jesus and His blood and dissociated from social and religious systems. Our sacrificial worship is 'the fruit of lips that confess His name', (13:15) in contrast to the physical sacrifices of 10:11 by the Aaronic priests. Whilst the physical sacrifice, even though costly cannot please the heart of God,

---

[90] Westcott B 2nd Ed 1892 The Epistle to the Hebrews: The Greek text with notes and essays Macmillan and Co Scotland

yet the service and communication of the believer to others in need is well pleasing to God (13:16).

In conclusion, external sacrifice and rituals are ineffective when presented to God as a way of appeasing His wrath at the sight of sin. Only the blood of Jesus our Lord could make us holy before our awesome Creator God.

Practical Exercise

1. *Note that throughout the book of Hebrews, the author has consistently used the word 'tabernacle' rather than the temple in Jerusalem. In the light of Heb 13:14 why do you think this is the case?*

2. *God's laws and sacrifices were intended to bring out true devotion of the heart but in fact they became external rituals of culture rather than belief in the one and only true and living God. What rituals can you see in the church today that have replaced worshipping God 'in spirit and in truth' (John 4:24)?*

3. *The Hebrews author adjured his audience not to 'be carried away by all kinds of strange teachings' (Heb 13:9). This refers to various Jewish food laws laid down by God at Sinai in Leviticus but which had been unnecessarily added to by subsequent priestly generations. These had all been wiped away through the death of Jesus on the cross which cleansed not only humans but also the animal world of their uncleanness. Read Romans 14 and reflect on whether you personally adhere unintentionally to certain 'food laws' which are either cultural, traditional or from peer pressure.*

NOTES

An Antidote to Carnal Religion

CHAPTER SEVENTEEN
CASE STUDIES

Your word is a lamp to my feet and a light to my path

Psalm 119:105

Biographical narrative enables the human story to be told in all its sordidness, sadness, and angst, yet also the joy in living life to the full when man obeys his Creator. Here we examine four life stories to see how those lives point to Jesus, 'the author and finisher of our faith' and where they fit into the immense plan that God has for His earth. Generations of the earth's population learn from their ancestors, each building on the learning blocks of the previous generation. So, God has given us, in His Word, ways for us to learn from our spiritual ancestors, descendants of the promise of Abraham (Rom 9:8).

At the end of each case study there is a practical exercise to enable further reflection and consolidate learning. For this purpose, they can be viewed as worked examples for the believer who wants to become a proficient user of the Bible.

Case Study A

Kadesh Barnea

Hebrews 3:7-19; Psalm 95:7-11; Numbers 13:1-14:12

This is the first of four specific Old Testament passages used by the writer of Hebrews which we want to look at in greater detail to see how he uses the interpreters' tools. It is important not to forget the primary purpose of bringing to the Jewish mind a transformative understanding of the person and work of Jesus Christ.

This first is primarily a word study which rests on the verbal inspiration of Scripture by the Holy Spirit. But there are other features of the interpretation which will be included.

The Quotation

The Hebrews author introduces the passage with his 'reading' of Psalm 95:7-11 (Heb 3:7-11), carefully attributing it to Divine Authorship, 'as the Holy Spirit says'. Let it be no mere formality when we say that we are reading God's Word, but rather be continually aware that it is the work of the Holy Spirit that interprets Scripture for us who read it (Heb 9:8; 10:15). Westcott[90] makes the point that the passage was not one favoured in temple ceremony, although used in synagogues, so it seems that the Hebrew interpreter knew his Scriptures well. Before reading these verses from Hebrews Wright[91] wants us to understand that the author is comparing his listeners to the wandering Israelites. We too are on a journey of unimaginable proportions that will eventually, through all the desert challenges, lead us to the Promised Land, heaven, and the place of rest.

Date of the Psalm

The Septuagint Greek translation of the Old Testament, which was made in Alexandria 200 years before Christ[92] is used by the Hebrews

---

[90] Westcott B 2nd Ed 1892 The Epistle to the Hebrews: The Greek text with notes and essays Macmillan and Co Scotland

[91] Wright T 2003 *Hebrews for Everyone* Published by Society for Promoting Christian Knowledge UK

author to quote Psalm 95:7-11 which ascribes the human authorship to David. This enables the writer to affirm that it postdates Joshua's conquests at the end of the wilderness journey (Heb 4:7) and therefore is a promise of rest which supersedes all that Canaan could offer.

Literal Meaning of the Psalm

We can go no farther until we are sure of the incident to which the Psalm is referring. This will need some careful research. Where was the 'provocation'(AV) 'rebellion' (NIV Heb 3:8) and when was 'the day of temptation' (AV) 'time of testing' (NIV)? Part of the search challenge is geographical, as is often the case when moving between two different eras. The Rock at Rephidim, Horeb, is called the same as the second rock at the other end of the journey (Num 20:13). Kadesh-Barnea is called variously the Desert of Paran; El Quseima; Kadesh; and later Qadesh-Barnea. It is found on the southern reaches of the Negev, on the south border of what was to become the kingdom of Judah. It is helpful to make visual connections by using a Bible atlas.

Meribah (meaning provocation or quarrelling) is used in the same context as Massah (Ex 17:7) which is the word for temptation[93]. Massah takes on a similar characteristic used elsewhere in Scripture: Deuteronomy 6:16; 9:22-23; 33:8. Kadesh-Barnea appears to be the significant place and day of provocation when the forty year 'loathing' or 'wrath' was passed on the people. They became the 'generation' who died in the wilderness (Heb 3:17; Num 14:29) all except Joshua and Caleb who were rewarded for their reliance on God. This is where a word study might be helpful.

This was the example of Hebrews 4:11, held up to demonstrate the consequences of unbelief, which led to judgement at the end of the relatively short journey from Egypt. Having spent nine months building the tabernacle and receiving the law from God, the Israelites

---

[92] Zuck, R 1991 *Basic Bible Interpretation: A Practical Guide to Discovering Biblical Truth* Victor Publishing USA UK

[93] Darby J 1961 New Translation Bible Stow Hill Bible and Tract Depot Kingston UK available at: www.biblegateway.com/versions/Darby-Translation-Bible/#booklist accessed Nov 2021

should have been settled in the Promised Land within two years. In contrast, the great burden of the epistle is that membership of the 'house' (which is Christ's) inevitably assumes the responsibility of holding 'onto our courage and the hope of which we boast' (Heb 3:6). It is wrong to hide this truth from the soul considering the claims of the Lord Jesus for the first time and the consequent responsibility that will be placed upon their faith in God.

The Gist of the Story of Kadesh Barnea

In paraphrasing scripture and owning the subject matter the student is able to discover the salient features as well as grasping the central point of the narrative. This shows that the student understands the passage and can move onto application. Using all the references to this narrative (Numbers 13:1-14:12; 32:6-13) we can give a short summary noting similar words:

The people of Israel had crossed the Desert of Paran after a very public display of discontent and judgment from Miriam and Aaron. The people made their way to their next encampment having seen God's punishment and then forgiveness after repentance. They were now on the brink of entering their promised 'rest' but first needed to spy out the land that they were going to take over. Each tribe was to send one leader who would represent them and 'spy out' the land which would belong to them.

They were given specific instructions by Moses: Travel through the Negev to the hill country. See whether the people are weak or strong, the population and the fertility of the land and soil. Observe the towns for fortifications and whether they are well built cities and villages. Look to see what kind of animals are living off the land and what trees or plants they are growing. Bring back with you some produce of the land.

The twelve men walked swiftly through the southern parts of the land, gathering information as they went. Returning through the Valley of Eschol they found giant grape clusters which could only be carried on poles between two men. Pomegranates and figs were in abundance and these they also brought back. However, on their return after forty days away, ten of the men started to focus on the physical strength of the unusually large people that they had encountered. As an aside they mentioned the abundant fertility of the land but moved on very quickly to tell how strong their fortifications were and the rumours they had heard of tribes along the Jordan and coastal routes. These were prime sites necessary for water and for travel and trade.

Caleb jumped in to say that of course the Israelites could take the land but was immediately silenced by the voice of the majority. This majority became perjurious and the people rebelled as a whole, looking back to Egypt as their country of choice. Joshua and Caleb stood up and told the truth about the land, recognising the faith in the protection of the Lord needed to 'swallow up' the present inhabitants. The key to this was to believe the Lord and His promises and not to rebel.

The situation descended into near murder of these faithful few until God stepped in and reminded them of his love and faithfulness. Because of their unbelief and rebellion, they would now have to suffer the consequences and travel the desert for forty years, one year for every day that the spies had spent in His Promised Land. These forty years represented a time of testing for the Israelites in the desert.

A similar situation arose another forty years later when they had arrived at the Jordan and once again it was unbelief in the previous generation of which Moses reminded them.

Notice how the writer of Hebrews grasped 'unbelief' to be the central point of the reversal in Israel's history at Kadesh-Barnea. He associates judgment with unbelief (Num 14:29; 26:64, 65) but draws attention to the exceptions, Joshua, and Caleb (what belief these men showed backsliding Israel, Num 14:7-9). Joshua and Caleb were one sixth of the company that set out to spy the land. The Biblical authors are familiar with the Bible theme of the faithful always being a minority, 'a remnant' (Rom 9:27; 11:5).

Using the Margins

To have worked through so far, the student will probably have used the marginal references to chase up parallel passages. Still keeping an eye on the margin of the Bible note that the Greek in Hebrews 3:11 reads 'if they shall enter into my rest'(AV) 'they shall never enter my rest' (NIV also Heb 4:5) compares with the marginal rendering of the Hebrew in Psalm 95:11 (see the original promise given in Ex 33:1,14). Was there a question mark over God's promise? Rather, the student must grasp the ways in which 'if' (AV) or 'never' (NIV) is used in Scripture.

Self-Questioning

Notice that in gaining the attention of his readers, the writer of Hebrews adopts an interrogatory method, the reader, hearer, disciple, or student is being questioned (Heb 3:17-18) 'with whom' and 'to whom'?). Indeed, when studying Scripture, we should continually be asking ourselves such questions.

Doctrinal Origins

A basic question arising from the Old Testament passage is, 'what is God's Rest?' This pre-dated Moses and Sinai and was introduced before there was a Hebrew race. It was the possession of God Himself on the basis of His completed creation. Creation was examined and found to be satisfactory to His own standards of perfection (Gen 2:2,3) and as a result made the seventh day holy because of the rest He found in perfection. The sabbath is referred on this occasion rather than to the Ten Commandments where it becomes law rather than principle. In studying, the student should be prepared to break off and meditate on glorious truths such as these with a heart full of worship.

The blessed, Divine Rest is one such subject. At Kadesh Barnea, this rest was denied to Israel. When Israel eventually entered Canaan, Joshua (watch the margin in case the Greek form of his name misleads you, Heb 4:8) proclaimed their rest (Josh 22:4), but our knowledge of Judges convinces us that Canaan never offered the antitypical rest of God's Sabbath. As the interpretation unfolds, the Hebrews writer is able to conclude that the offer from God is still standing: 'there remains then, a Sabbath rest for the people of God' (Heb 4:9). Although the rest had been available from creation, subsequent dispensations had not made it real to the people of God. It needed the Saviour from heaven and the work of the Spirit to bring it within grasp. As faith stands in contrast to unbelief, so it contrasts with works (Heb 4:10) and results from the Gospel (Heb 4:2). The interpretation concludes with an exhortation in the form of an unforgettable conundrum, 'Let us, therefore, make every effort to enter that rest' (Heb 4:11).

The Word Study

Directly after his quotation of Psalm 95, the writer takes the word, 'today', as a call to immediacy (Heb 3:13-15). He tells the readers to exercise themselves 'daily' in mutual exhortation to avoid becoming hardened sinners. Leaving Egypt, like the Christian's meeting with the Living God, was a sudden experience. 'Hardening our hearts' is a process which can extend from the Red Sea to Kadesh-Barnea, and a daily corrective of fellowship would be an excellent insurance for the believer's confidence to remain 'steadfast to the end'.

Returning to the word 'today', the author says it is a particular day, a day when the opportunity is again opened for the people of God (Heb 4:9). Furthermore, it was not in that day of Israel's provocation but long after, in David's psalm. It is a day when all those who believe in the Lord Jesus Christ can cease from their works and enter the rest of God, the same rest that God had on the seventh day of creation.

The interpreter has been so impressed with the power of the passage to exhort the readers, that he breaks out in a postscript (Heb 4:12-13) which worships the immutable Creator God who is all seeing, all knowing, all powerful. This is not a normal postscript in that it introduces a whole new subject reminding the student that the Word of God cuts open the heart, examining it in every detail with a view to transforming it to be like Christ.

Practical Exercise

1. *Go back over the story of Kadesh Barnea (Numbers 13:1-14:12; 32:6-13) to see if you come to the same conclusion as the author of Hebrews that the underlying sin of Israel was unbelief (compare Num 14:11 with Heb 4:11). What other themes can you draw out from the narrative?*

2. *In what ways would an understanding of the geography, culture, and language enable the reader to interpret the narrative at Kadesh-Barnea?*

3. *Examine the ways in which believer's are kept from 'entering God's rest' by revisiting Hebrews 3:11; 4:3,11, and the apparent opposite in Exodus 33:5,14.*

NOTES

God Speaks

Case Study B

Melchizedek, The King of Salem

Hebrews 5:8, 13-20; 7 - 8:2; Psalm 110:1,4; Genesis 14:18-20

Our second case study is a scripture biography of the man known as Melchizedek King of Salem pronounced *mal-kee-tseh'-dek*.

The Quotation

It is evident that the quotation and interpretation of Psalm 110 formed something of a framework for the whole epistle. This was not an unusual occurrence in first century writings as Ps 110 is the most quoted Psalm in the New Testament[94] possibly because this may have been used regularly as a hymn. The first verse of the Psalm is only quoted by the writer of Hebrews in 1:13, elsewhere he simply alludes to it (Heb 1:9; 10:12,13; 12:2). Once again, we see that he is very selective in the passage he will interpret. Although so much of the psalm is instructive, he restrains himself to deal with verses 1 and 4 alone. This is a good example to follow as to the wise selectiveness of a passage to interpret. Notice too that there are differences between his quotation and Psalm 110:4 (see 5:10; 6:20; 10:21; and 7:28). That the psalm is messianic is stated by the Lord Jesus and agreed by the Pharisees (Matt 22:41-46) as well as preached apostolically (Acts 2:34).

In contrast, the verse from Psalm 110 is quoted six times during its interpretation. Heb 5:6,10; 6:20; 7:17, 21, 28. Although it is only a single verse, the writer does not even quote the whole of it until he needs to in 7:1 (also 5:6). The last reference is more of a paraphrase joining with 8:1 as the summary which is to linger in the readers minds. The first two quotations are chiefly to introduce Melchizedek as a man and challenge the readers as to their stage in development of scripture study.

---

[94] Dillehay J 2020 Jesus according to the New Tetament's most quoted Psalm available at: www.thegospelcoalition.org/article/psalm-110/ accessed Nov 2021

Notice how in Heb 5:10; 6:20 the Holy Spirit sanctions the author to write 'High Priest' rather than 'priest': an ordinary priest would have been a much weaker type of the Lord Jesus in all His priestly functions towards us and our God (see too Heb 3:1; 7:28 and 10:21 'great' priest in NIV: 4:14; 9:11). One way of going through the case study would be to see what additional interpretation is made with each successive quotation of Psalm 110:4.

Interpretation

Few interpreters today would be able to do a study of the character, Melchizedek, without digressing fancifully on the mysteries that surround him including the intriguing subject of theophanies (a visible manifestation of God). But would these have added to the thrust of the writers' interpretation and exhortation? We can be quite sure that the author enjoyed the remembrance of the Lord Jesus by breaking bread as much as we do yet he tried to draw no lesson from the bread and wine which Melchizedek brought out to the victorious company of Abraham (Gen 14:18). This is one of the great values of narrative Scripture, that it is more easily retained in our memories, and consequently the Holy Spirit can use it in public or private instruction without recourse to deep Biblical study.

However, the writer does search the Old Testament to find and use all the other information (Gen 14:18-20) about the character he is studying. He also uses Melchizedek to challenge (Heb 5:10-14) the readers' low performance in Scripture knowledge and use as we saw in Heb 1:5,14.

Melchizedek's office was both King and Priest of God Most High. Choosing or appointing priests is God's sole prerogative, such as Aaron (Heb 5:4) and also applies to ourselves (1 Pet 2:9; Rev 5:10) and to the Lord Jesus who was 'designated by God to be High Priest' (Heb 5:10). Consider whether Gethsemane was the test of the Son of God for His suitability for the office (Heb 5:7-8). Heb 5:10 suggests that the Lord Jesus was named High Priest of God subsequent to His obedience (suffering v8, prayers v7, completion v9 and His work as Saviour v 9). Does it follow that the hermeneutical standard of 'solid food' (Heb 5:14) relates to appreciating the Lord's present office rather than the doctrine of salvation? It sounds as though the student who shows proficiency in following the writer's interpretation of Melchizedek graduates from student to teacher.

The Lord Jesus can be distinguished as our Great High Priest, first because He has right of access into the most Holy Place and secondly because He stays there, seated into eternity, which Aaron never could.

Typology

If you or I took up an incident or character as a type of the Lord, we could easily lead people to wrong comparisons with that Blessed Person if we did not make out a clear case to justify our typology. Does the writer make a clear case here for Melchizedek as a type?

The first proof of his case is that the author is using a declared Messianic Psalm as the basis of his interpretation: the context of the verse concerns 'My Lord'. The next might be that the author is describing an eternal Being and position: 'A priest for ever'. Incidentally, this means that the lack of a genealogy for the historical King of Salem is not merely a fanciful position as 'like the Son of God he remains a priest forever (Heb 7:3) which establishes the basis for seeing Melchizedek as a type. Then again, the Psalm clearly looks forward to another of the class or order of Melchizedek, and only the Lord Jesus will fit that role. Genesis 14 is also shown to prove the appropriateness of the Lord Jesus as Melchizedek's antitype by titles: King of righteousness; King of Peace. The gospels abound with testimonies to the Lord's regal status and His life, and accomplishments in death show that righteousness and peace have never so aptly described a man on earth or in the glory.

The dual tasks of the priest as blesser and receiver of the tokens of practical worship (tithes) were shown from Genesis 14 and provide such a link with all that our Blessed Lord is now doing that surely no doubt can remain as to how appropriately Hebrews uses Melchizedek as a type.

Just as Moses was warned expressly not to deviate from the heavenly pattern when the tabernacle was constructed (Ex 25:40; Heb 8:5), so the Lord Jesus must be the clear and unique antitype of Melchizedek. If we ask, 'Was King Saul's impatience (1 Sam 13:9-14) both understandable and rather trivial for God's wrath and Samuel's behaviour towards him? The answer must be, 'No', because God chooses the priest as He did the Aaronic line (Ex 28:1) and here was the very first King of Israel, with the extra responsibilities that entailed, assuming priestly functions as well as regal. In the same way Ps 110:4 and Heb 5:5 show that Christ was also chosen and called by God.

Similarly (2 Chron 26:16-23) King Uzziah in his pride attempted to offer incense as a priest. How well the priest understood the distinct roles: 'it is not right for you, Uzziah, to burn incense to the Lord. That is for the priests of the descendants of Aaron, who have been consecrated to burn incense.' Leprosy sprang up in his forehead instead of a crown on his head. Unlike Miriam's leprosy (Num 12:1-15) there was no reprieve. How much light this throws on Isaiah 6:1-5, where Uzziah's death as a leper is contrasted with the divine and regal person worthy of worship who has the unique authority of sitting in the incense filled temple. This is the antitype of whom Hebrews speaks. You notice that the priests in Uzziah's day, together with their high priest, point to their consecration as their right to offer incense (and much else). Uzziah lacked this, furthermore he adjudged himself to be worthy of performing as a priest (contrast with Heb 5:4). No priest, apart from Melchizedek, was given regal authority, so although Uzziah assumed a priestly duty the crown still passed to his son Jotham (2 Chron 26:23) as King only.

However, rather than just making the statement that Melchizedek is a type of the Lord Jesus, the student would do well to justify this through the various methods mentioned above. To do this we need to return to the six characteristics of types and answer the question that follows each one:

Remembering that the antitype is the heightened version of a type, what are the resemblances or similarities between Melchizedek and Christ?

1. *Was the figure of Melchizedek in Genesis 14:18-20 a historical reality?*
2. *As 'type' is a form of prophecy pointing towards things yet to*

come, is Melchizedek a foreshadowing or prediction of Christ?
3. Is the antitype, Christ, greater than Melchizedek?
4. As in the pattern created by God for the tabernacle in the wilderness, which was to be copied exactly as God stated, does the likeness between Melchizedek and Christ have the same imprint of Divine design?
5. Has the New Testament designated this type and antitype between Melchizedek and Christ?

Each of the above questions requires further study and referencing in order to show the robustness of the student's research and the consequent depth of understanding gained from the book of Hebrews. As these questions are explored so the reality of Christ will emerge with an even greater understanding, just as the Hebrews author meant to convey to his listeners.

The writer proves the appropriateness of identifying Melchizedek as a type of the Lord Jesus by the title King of Salem (righteousness and peace). Thus, we see how the type is 'made like unto the Son of God' (the pattern).

Wright[95] states that a study of the story of Melchizedek in relation to Christ has the effect of a lighthouse, sending rays of light flashing over the rest of Hebrews bringing the text and more importantly, Christ, to life. It leads us to many other texts in the Bible, particularly Psalm 110 and so to the Messiah, heightening our desire for knowing more about the wonderful Author and Finisher of our faith.

The Purpose of the Biographical Study

There are very many characters in Scripture which we, or the author of Hebrews, might choose to study in depth. A valuable purpose could arise as we continue our investigations, but surely, we should not finish up with merely the 'Official Biography of ....'. The author of Hebrews gives us the biography of Melchizedek because he saw that this character typified the Lord Jesus in His role now as King and High

---

[95] Wright T 2003 *Hebrews for Everyone* Published by Society for Promoting Christian Knowledge UK

Priest. This is why, for instance, he glides over the beautiful words of the blessings which Melchizedek pronounced (Gen 14:19-20) and of, course, says nothing of the King of Sidon hovering like a vulture in the background.

Finally, what application should we draw from this study of a little-known man in the Old Testament who is given such space in this book of Hebrews? The fact that we know a greater High Priest than the King of Salem should surely make our hearts beat faster with praise and worship for this one who has brought salvation to all those who are waiting for Him.

Practical Exercise

1. *Read Justin Dillehay's[96] commentary on Psalm 110 https://www.thegospelcoalition.org/article/psalm-110/ and reflect on the methods that he used to unpick this much used 'hymn'.*

2. *The testimony of believers is the most effective and articulate way of witnessing today, pointing away from themselves and towards the Lord Jesus. There are many Christian testimonies online today and conferences that use this method to inspire believers to go into short term or full-time work for the Lord. The Keswick Convention is one such platform and can be accessed online at https://keswickministries.org/ . There are also many radio programmes that are dedicated to Christian testimony for instance www.heartofthematter.biz . Use one of these to listen to the stories and be inspired and captivated by the way in which personal lives can point to Jesus Christ.*

3. *Melchizedek points us to the greater High Priest, Jesus Christ. What verses stand out for you in this case study that makes you want to apply this teaching in your Christian life? What have you done or are considering doing that is motivated by love for your fellow human being and will point towards Christ and not yourself?*

---

[96] Dillehay J 2020 Jesus according to the New Tetament's most quoted Psalm available at: www.thegospelcoalition.org/article/psalm-110/ accessed Nov 2021

NOTES

Case Study C

The comparison of Old and New Testament quotes in Hebrews

Heb 8:6-10:18 Jeremiah 31:31-34

This case study examines the use of quotations, translations, commentaries, and typology.

As before we look first at the author's quotation (the longest in the letter) from the Old Testament (Heb 8:8-12). Apart from differences in punctuation, verse 12 in the AV expands the original Hebrew somewhat, and the Holy Spirit has allowed an additional clause as well as one clause to be omitted:

'For I will be merciful to their unrighteousness, and their sins and their iniquities will I remember no more' Heb 8:12 AV.

'For I will forgive their iniquity, and I will remember their sin no more' Jer 31:34 AV.

Interestingly, the NIV repeats the same words in both Jeremiah and Hebrews:

'For I will forgive their wickedness and will remember their sins no more' Jer 31:34; Heb 8:12.

The Message, however, is a little understated in its translation of being forgiven, one of the shortcomings of a paraphrase:

'They'll get to know me by being kindly forgiven, with the slate of their sins forever wiped clean' Heb 8:12.

In these verses the quotation has been introduced by the writer comparing the tasks of the Lord and Moses relative to God's Covenants. The 'faulty' (finding fault with them plainly refers to the people who attempted to keep to the first covenant Heb 8:8) covenant administered by Moses and needing replacement, indicated the inferiority of this first covenant compared with the New Covenant instituted by Christ (Luke 22:20).

170

Case Study C Comparison of Old and New Testament
quotes from Hebrews

Turning to commentaries we find that cross references from an online commentary such as e-Sword can enable the student to look across the whole of Scripture when interpreting this particular passage:

Heb 10:16-17; Psalm 25:7, Psalm 65:3; Isa 43:25, Isa 44:22; Jer 33:8, Jer 50:20; Mic 7:19; Act 13:38-39; Rom 11:27; Eph 1:7; Col 1:14; 1Jn 1:7-9, 1Jn 2:1-2; Rev 1:5.

The commentary from e-Sword[97] however falls a little short on the explanation of each verse, so it is helpful to examine other commentaries such as Sonic Light[98]:

Hebrews 8:8-12 God gave the promise of a new covenant because the people of Israel had failed Him. He also did so because the Old Mosaic Covenant did not have the power to enable them to remain faithful to God. The New Covenant includes the power whereby God's people may remain faithful, namely: the presence of God living within the believer (i.e., the Holy Spirit). This is one way in which it differs from the Old Covenant (v. 9).

How great is the contrast between the old and the new covenant! In the one God demands of sinful man: 'Thou shalt.' In the other God promises: 'I will.'

The writer used the Greek word 'kainos' to describe this covenant. Kainos means different in quality as well as new in time, as opposed to simply new in point of time, which the Greek word 'neos' describes. The New Covenant has not only been given more recently than the Old Covenant, but it is of a different, superior quality.

God promised that the New Covenant would enable the Israelites to do four things: They would (1) know and desire to do God's will ("I will put My laws into their minds, and ... write them on their hearts"; v. 10b), (2) enjoy a privileged, unique relationship with God ("I will be their God, and they shall be My people"; v. 10c), (3) "know" God ("the

---

[97] Available at https://www.e-sword.net/ accessed November 2021

[98] Sonic Light 2021 Bible Commentary Dr Thomas Constable available at https://www.planobiblechapel.org/tcon/notes/html/nt/hebrews/hebrews.htm accessed November 2021

171

Lord") directly (v. 11), and (4) experience permanent forgiveness of their sins ("I will be merciful … and … remember their sins no more"; v. 12). (A double negative in the Greek text of verse 12 heightens this promise: "I will never, ever remember their sins.") These are the "better [i.e., unconditional] promises" the writer referred to earlier (v. 6).

'… new covenant promises are not yet fully realized. The promises in Jeremiah, Isaiah, and Ezekiel describe a people who have the law written in their hearts, who walk in the way of the Lord, fully under the control of the Holy Spirit. These same promises look to a people who are raised from the dead [cf. Ezek. 37], enjoying the blessings of an eternal inheritance with God dwelling with them and in them forever'.

Wright[99] in his commentary, emphasises the importance of the different phases of Hebrews following on from each other *'forming one long single argument'. 'Just as Psalm 95 continued to be the vital text in chapters 3 and 4, and Psalm 110 from chapter 5 to the middle of chapter 8, so Jeremiah 31 continues to be in the writer's mind, and should be in yours as well, all the way from this point to the end of chapter 10.'* Wright's application here is important because he gives these verses as a 'powerful argument' which look to Jesus rather than the legalism of Judaism, for to do so, he contends, would be both foolish and disloyal.

We see here the usefulness of consulting different translations and commentaries when interpreting the Word of God. None of them give a full exposition of the passage on their own but put together the Holy Spirit can then speak into the reader's need for a particular hermeneutic required at the time.

It is in Hebrews 9 that the principles of typology are set out by the Holy Spirit. The purpose is given (v8) as a significant illustration to the people of the tabernacle dispensation, *'The present time (v9)',* that God was unapproachable even with their sacrifices and gifts awaiting the coming of the Lord Jesus for reformation. Those people were left with uneasy consciences (v10): quite unlike the purge of consciences

---

[99] Wright T 2003 *Hebrews for Everyone* Published by Society for Promoting Christian Knowledge UK

Case Study C Comparison of Old and New Testament
quotes from Hebrews

(9:14) which the new type of High Priest has brought in.

It has often been perplexing to the Bible student to see how the writer passed from the idea of a covenant to the Greek word for a testament (virtually 'a will') where the effect of the need for death is self-evident. The blood sacrifice at the inauguration of the first Covenant (Heb 9:21-23; Ex 24:4-8) is seen as a poor analogy for the testators' death (Heb 9:15-18). Even if the sanctification of the 'patterns' (Heb 9:23) clearly requires such a sacrifice and precious blood as given at Calvary, this is both unrepeatable and needs no repetition (Heb 9:24-28). Then a further challenge facing the student is that whereas the promise through Jeremiah was to Israel, the author of Hebrews sees no such restriction (Heb 9:28; 12:23).

This case study is an excellent starting point for the Bible student to make a complete Scripture study of the topic of Covenants. It will prove far from sterile in that it will bring out more heart affection for the Saviour who said, 'this is my blood of the [New] covenant (Matt 26:28; Mark 14:24; Luke 22:20; 1 Cor 11:25). The contrast of what is 'New' with what and why it is 'Old' will also provide a useful lead into study.

Many Christians today pay little attention to types, but God placed great emphasis on their conforming to His will. It is in this way that the story of the rock at Meribah (Num 20:13) should be understood. The punishment of Moses for smiting instead of speaking to the rock all hinged on sanctifying the person of God (Deut 3:26; 32:51).

The punishment of Uzziah (Azariah) was similar in that, had he been allowed to act as a priest whilst King of Judah, he would have pre-empted the place of Christ (Ps 110:1-4; Heb10:5 ff; Is 6:1ff; 2 Chron 26:16-21; 2 Kings 15:5ff). Even the priests of Uzziah's day understood the enormity of his crime. Notice all the contrasts between this self-appointed King-priest and the Lord.

The student is helped to grasp the typological teaching of the tabernacle by the contrast between everything that kept people out (Heb 9:8) and the invitation to draw near (Heb 10:19-22).

Practical Exercise

1. *From the various translations that you have chosen to use, what are the differences between them when looking at Hebrews 8:7-13? Discover why the further quotation (10:16, 17) is different and what the significance of this is to our understanding of the passage. The AV adds 'after' (10:15) and 'before' (10:15). To what do you think this refers?*

2. *Using an e-commentary of your choice, list the common denominators between these passages, following them through in the light of the Hebrews author's own comments from chapters 8-10: Psalm 25:7; Psalm 65:3; Isaiah 43:25; Isaiah 44:22; Jeremiah 33:8; Jeremiah 50:20; Micah 7:19; Acts 13:38-39; Romans 11:27; Ephesians 1:7; Colossians 1:14; 1 John 1:7-9, 1 John 2:1-2; Revelation 1:5.*

3. *Source a readable hardback commentary of your choice on Hebrews and note down all the areas that had not previously occurred to you on your first reading of Hebrews 8-10.*

NOTES

Case Study C Comparison of Old and New Testament quotes from Hebrews

Case Study D

The Beauty of Holiness: Jehoshaphat and the Anatomy of Sanctification

Heb 10:11-18;12:5-8 1 Kings 22:1-50

This case study traverses bibliography, word study and application in its interpretation of the little-known story of Jehoshaphat, one of the Kings of Judah.

There are twenty-eight references to Jehoshaphat in the Old Testament, the final one (Joel 3:2,12) a geographical reference, showing the importance of this king to the history of the Jews and their relationship to God. Somewhere in this narrative there is an application for us today.

The chronicler tells us that Jehoshaphat's mother's name was Azubah the daughter of Shilhi (1 Kings 22:42,43) and we can assume that his godliness was in no small part due to her training as well as his father Asa. The mother of Jehoshaphat's children is not mentioned for unusually, the Holy Spirit does not supply her name, and we cannot but think that she played a part in the family tragedy. Mothers have a remarkable influence over the direction that their children walk in: Timothy (2 Tim 1:5); Sarah (1 Pet 3:6); Ruth (4:15).

Separation from the world – The process of sanctification

Jehoshaphat was 35 years old when he followed Asa on the throne of Judah and took his stand against the idolatrous nation of Israel his northern neighbour. Israel had been ruled for four years by Ahab and his Baal-worshipping consort, Jezebel. Ahab and Jezebel's children followed their idol worship eventually murdering each other all except one little boy (2 Kings 11:1,2). The king of Judah, however, maintained the enmity of his predecessors towards Israel and strengthened his border towns (2 Chron 17:1-6). He neither copied his godless neighbours, nor desired their Baalim.

Jehoshaphat reigned for twenty-five years and during that time, the process of his sanctification can be traced as a proactive measure against the evil that was going on in all the countries around Judah. He actively sought God and boasted in God's ways. Paul the apostle writes similarly, *'May I never boast except in the cross of our Lord Jesus Christ'* (Gal 6:14). Judah in consequence was blessed by the Lord with peace and honour among the nations (2 Chron 17:5).

The word 'sanctification' has often been translated by the NIV as 'being made holy' (Heb 10:10,14; 1 Cor 1:30). Romans 5:2; 15:16 describe the process of becoming more and more like Jesus Christ through the work of the Holy Spirit as *sanctification*. There are three basic changes that God makes in the lives of believers in order to become more like him:

1. Becoming free from sin's control: We died to sin (Rom 6:2) and have become free (v7) from sin, but alive to God and therefore able to offer all the parts of our bodies that we have been using for sin, back to God (v11-14).

2. Recognising and dealing with the continuing lifetime struggle over sin: Understanding the laws of God to recognise sin (Rom 7:7) in our lives and allowing God to deal with it (v24) on a regular basis (Rom 12:1).

3. God gives us the victory over sin: He reminds us that all our sin is forgiven and there is no condemnation, therefore no guilt for anything done in the past (Rom 8:1). His Spirit lives in us and frees us from fear (v15), knowing that we will never be separated from the love of Christ (v 35). Consequently 'in all these things we are more than conquerors through him who loved us (v 37)'.

Jehoshaphat's life traced the work of sanctification throughout his reign, but not without many challenges that seemed to take him away from God's eternal purpose for Israel. After all, as Kings and governors appointed by God (Ps 2) they are set in place by God who sees the end from the beginning yet allows them to go so far and no further.

Separation from Evil

Sanctification is not concerned with external relations alone, but with what a believer is in himself. Thus, Jehoshaphat set the affairs of Judah

177

on a godly course. He removed the high places and groves (2 Chron 17:6), though just as the Christian discovers cells of resistance in his heart, 'The people offered and burnt incense yet in the high places' (1 Kings 22:43). Homosexuality is a barometer of the moral state of a nation so Jehoshaphat rid the land of male shrine-prostitutes, known as sodomites (1 Kings 22:46; 1 Thess 4:3-8). The book of the law of the Lord became well known to the people of Judah (2 Chron 17:7-9) through a specific programme of teaching using the law of God. Jesus told the disciples (John 17:17) that they were to do the same and, in this way, believers would be made holy, as long as it was the truth that was being taught. This was reiterated by Paul (Eph 5:26) when he showed the love of Christ for the church and His desire to 'make her holy'.

Later King Jehoshaphat himself itinerated through Judah to revive the worship of God (2 Chron 19:4), so earnestly did he seek the sanctification of his people when they had strayed from God's Word. Spiritual purity and righteous living go hand in hand for a sanctified believer. So it was that Jehoshaphat established righteousness with a god-fearing judiciary throughout Judah (2 Chron 19:5-11). Impartiality, faithfulness, justice, and courage had to characterize the men chosen by the king. The members of the Body of Christ need to show these same attributes, especially Overseers, Elders, Deacons or whoever are appointed to serve in God's church. For maintaining law and order within, and to defend the kingdom, Jehoshaphat had trusted and experienced warriors (2 Chron 17:13-19). One at least, Amasiah, first and foremost dedicated himself to the Lord (v16). Though the weapons of our warfare are not carnal (Eph 6:12), our sanctification is a real conflict.

The Holy War

Jehoshaphat fought one of the most amazing Bible battles, recorded in 2 Chronicles 20. His intelligence service reported the massing of Moabites and their allies on the shores of the Dead Sea. In natural fear he prayed, and the nation fasted. The king threw himself on the faithfulness of God to His promises. This sanctified man always respected the prophets of the Lord and perhaps this was why God consistently sent His messengers to Jehoshaphat. On this occasion

Jahaziel encouraged Judah with the word from God: Do not be afraid or discouraged because of this vast army. For the battle is not yours, but God's (v15)'. Unquestioningly, the king on hearing this with the people worshipped and praised. Jehoshaphat led Judah to implicit trust: 'Have faith in the Lord your God and you will be upheld; have faith in his prophets and you will be successful (v20)'. The army set forward to a song of praise: 'Give thanks to the Lord for his love endures forever (v21)'. Perhaps together they sang Psalm 136, echoing that line of praise after every statement of joy in the Lord their God. Surely there has never been such a distinctive body of soldiers: their joy and strength arose from their sanctification from all evil to the Lord, and this was expressed in the subject of their praise, 'The splendour of His Holiness'. Though it may be questioned what form of English most accurately gives the sense of the phrase, the people clearly appreciated the thrill of being the Lord's alone. After the victory, an incredible spoil was gathered. The people assembled in the valley of Beracah to bless the Lord, and in Jerusalem Jehoshaphat, who had so promoted the sanctification of God's people, led the praises.

Sanctification Compromised

Could this be the same man who 'made peace with the king of Israel' (1 Kings 22:44)? Blessed by God with material wealth, Jehoshaphat allied himself to Ahab (2 Chron 18:1), which seems to mean that he made a marriage for himself from Ahab's family, or it may refer to the marriage of his oldest son Jehoram to Athaliah, Ahab's daughter. It is true that through all the compromises which Jehoshaphat made, he never worshipped the idols of Israel nor renounced his faith in God. Did he think that he could influence Ahab for good by compromising his own sanctification? How many believers have thus rationalized an unequal yoke, compromising God's blessing!

Now it so happens that as he had heard Elijah's pronouncement in Naboth's vineyard, Ahab had been genuinely converted as attested by God (1 Kings 21:17-29). But Jezebel remained his consort. Did Jehoshaphat think that Ahab's change of heart was the result of his unholy alliance with the king of Israel and did this encourage him to go further and make a complete identification with Ahab for the battle of Ramoth Gilead? Though we must never breed disunity, it

179

is sometimes necessary to be careful in our relations with professed believers for they can lead us away from the Lord if they are not living according to God's Word. Wooed by Ahab's lavish hospitality and persuasion (2 Chron 18:2), Jehoshaphat became his ally, involving himself, all of Judah, and even his horses (1 Kings 22:4). As he had led Judah to holiness, now he led them to the loss of their sanctification. Just as surely as we can gain holiness so our actions can lead to a loss of holiness. This is the basis of Paul's plea to us in Romans 12:1,2.

Individual spiritual wellbeing or otherwise inevitably involves the whole church congregation. It is true Jehoshaphat tried to influence Ahab. He wanted to know the Lord's will before proceeding (2 Chron 18:4). He detected the hollowness of Ahab's massed prophets (2 Chron 18:6), and gently rebuked the king of Israel for despising the word from God if it did not suit his inclinations (2 Chron 18:7). But Jehoshaphat was silent when Micaiah warned of the consequences of the battle, and when the prophet was sentenced to bread and water in prison (2 Chron 18:26). On the battlefield Jehoshaphat was mistaken for Ahab (2 Chron 18:29-32), but the grace of God stepped in, and instead of perishing with Ahab, God drew the enemy away.

Whereas we are commanded by the Lord to be sanctified and holy (1 Pet 1:15-16), in our failure He does not desert us, but forgives and restores. This is clearly seen in the sequel to the battle of Ramoth-Gilead. Defeated, Jehoshaphat retired to Jerusalem to be met by a godly man, Jehu, with the words, *'Should you help the wicked and love those who hate the Lord? Because of this, the wrath of the Lord is upon you'* (2 Chron 19:1-3). The Lord does indeed discipline those He loves (Heb 12:5-8). Jehu recorded that the grace of God took account of Jehoshaphat's works and motives. To his credit, the king accepted Jehu's remonstration, unlike King Asa who imprisoned Hanani, Jehu's father, for his faithful prophecy (2 Chron 16:7-10). It must have been a pleasure for Jehu to have become Jehoshaphat's biographer (2 Chron 20:34).

We are all problem children and learn so slowly to walk with our Lord. In this narrative, Jehoshaphat next joined himself with Ahaziah (Ahab's older son) king of Israel, 'who was guilty of wickedness (2 Chron 20:35-37)'. The king of Judah showed his sanctified heart by refusing the alliance at first (1 Kings 22:49). He then gave in and accepted Israel as partners in a naval venture. Another prophet, Eliezer, condemned this unequal yoke, and the ships Jehoshaphat built were destroyed by the Lord (1 Kings 22:48; 2 Cor 6:14-18).

After Ahaziah's short and wicked reign over Israel, his brother Jehoram took over the kingdom and soon sent to Jehoshaphat for help to quell the Moabite rebellion (2 Kings 3:5-7). Had the king forgotten that previous holy war with Moab and the glorious victory? It looks as if the alliance he had made with the house of Ahab was still working out its deadly venom, because Jehoshaphat was at this time probably sharing the throne of Judah with his son, Jehoram, who was son-in-law to Ahab. The king of Judah's failure to keep separate from the evil was the mirror image of his previous sin over the battle of Ramoth Gilead. Again, he allied himself, his kingdom, and his horses with Israel. It could not be a successful adventure, and, late in the day, Jehoshaphat sought the Lord (2 Kings 3:11). Elisha clearly distinguished between the godly king of Judah and his companions (2 Kings 3:14). Once again God graciously delivered Jehoshaphat and gave victory over Moab.

Jehoshaphat may have enjoyed the Lord's forgiveness and restoration, he may have *'walked in the ways that his father David had followed'* (2 Chron 17:3), but the effects of his failure to remain sanctified from the surrounding evil brought the nation into disrepute after his death, and the house of David and lineage of Christ near extinction. He named his son after Ahab's son; his grandson was named after Ahab's elder son (his uncle). Murder, war, and defeat were the inheritance of Jehoshaphat's family.

Fellow believer, shall we exchange the Beauty of Holiness for an alliance with the world, its gods, and systems, without regard to the consequences to ourselves and those we love in the Lord?

Practical Exercise

1. *Can you trace the three basic changes that God made in Jehoshaphat's life when he became King which enabled his sanctification?*

2. *How was it that the reign of a king whose actions were summarized as 'doing that which was right in the eyes of the Lord' (1 Kings 22:43), led to a bloodbath among Jehoshaphat's children and grandchildren?*

3. *Some of Jehoshaphat's decisions seemed to contradict God's plan for Judah and Israel, but also interfered with the process of sanctification in his own life. What were those decisions and what was the impact that they had on Judah?*

4. *Apply the verse in Romans 'in all these things we are more than conquerors through him who loved us' (Rom 8:37) to your life right now. Reflect on what 'all these things' could be and trace the work that God is doing in your life over the years since you became a Christian.*

5. *Do we earnestly seek the sanctification of the people (2 Chron 19:1-7) in the church that we have been placed in and how should we go about it?*

6. *According to 2 Chron 20:21 the soldiers of the army of Jehoshaphat went to war with the praises of God on their lips. As believers in the same God, do we also carry with us the 'splendour of His Holiness' as we go about our God appointed work? If we do, how does that translate into our everyday lives?*

NOTES

182

Case Study D Jehoshaphat and the beauty of Holiness

Chapter Eighteen
The Matter before the Method

I will instruct you and teach you in the way you should go; I will counsel you and watch over you

Psalm 32:8

The Matter before the Method

In drawing this 'short guide to interpreting the Bible' to a conclusion we must assess as to what extent we have fitted ourselves for the Master's use in the handling of His Word. I am in danger of making out that the Epistle to the Hebrews is an exercise in scripture interpretation for its own sake. This is far from the truth. The author had a vital objective worthy of its place among the books of the Bible. He uses interpretation to prove his points, and this method will prove instructive to us because, with the completed scriptures in our hands, their interpretation is our chief bastion against errors of doctrine, behaviour, and practice. The interpreter always needs an objective. It is precisely because he has a particular purpose in his use of the Old Testament, that the author of Hebrews so strictly confines himself to appropriate scriptures and is by no means exhaustive in interpreting the earlier writers, even although he points the way for us.

It is probably impossible to look at the author's methods without any regard at all to the matter engaging him and quite wrong to ignore his aim in writing the letter. It is, however, difficult to deal with his subject adequately without digressing seriously from our avowed task. Then again, the subject of Hebrews presents so many contentions for those who revel in them, that we have to remember many arguments are unprofitable for us to tackle. In any case there are excellent commentaries which deal with the contents and background of the epistle that we would only add a shallow resume of them to the library shelf.

The following questions will enable the Bible student to grasp the contents of the epistle without falling into the difficulties of a fuller treatment I have just outlined.

The Author

How do the contents of Hebrews justify entitling it an Epistle?

After confirming and reinforcing doctrines set out elsewhere in the New Testament what does the author go on to explore?

What does the author say about himself that gives clues to his identity?

Is the commonly ascribed title to the book sufficient to think that the author is Paul and is that relevant?

What revelations of doctrine or practice does he give and what use does the author make of his authority to point us towards thinking that he is an apostle?

How would you use any knowledge you have of the author's identity?

First Readers

Were these first century readers called Hebrews anywhere in the letter?

Is the familiarity with the Old Testament expected by the author sufficient evidence to say they were Hebrews? [notice especially Hebrews 8:1,2 and 13:9-13]

What does the authors' referring to 'fathers' or 'forefathers' (1:1), 'elders' or 'ancients' (11:2) and 'brothers' (2:11-17; 3:1) suggest about the epistles recipients?

Does the writer suggest that the recipients ever had a personal experience of living under the old covenant?

Which passages show that the first readers were returning to Mosaic law and ceremony?

Who and where are the apostates amongst the readers specifically mentioned? What is the relevance of this to us? What can we learn from them?

List the words which are used to describe the danger of failure by the readers. What does this list convey to you?

Structure of the Book

Hebrews has been divided into a Doctrinal (hortatory) section: 1:1 – 10:18 and a didactic (or practical) section: 10:19 – 13:17. How is this useful?

There are five warning passages in Hebrews: give the references for these. How do they relate to the author's interpretation of Old Testament Scriptures.

What proportion of the whole epistle comprises the warning (numbers of verses for instance)? How should that affect us?

What do you draw from the fact that the epistle neither begins nor ends with one of the warning passages? And why are they not grouped together?

Relate the first six short exhortations in Hebrew 13 and the second six to the exclamation that separates them (13:8).

Comparison with other Epistles

Why is it commonly asserted that the Epistle to the Galatians is the closest parallel to Hebrews in the New Testament?

What are the main distinctions between Galatians and Hebrews according to the author's experiences, the origin, the subject of false teaching and the use of the Old Testament?

Notice the parallels in the following pairs of Scriptures: Gal 3:11 and Heb 10:38; Gal 2:21 and Heb 7:11; Gal 3:3 and Heb 6:4; Gal 3:4 and Heb 10:32-36; Gal 3:17 and Heb 6:12; Gal 4:9 and Heb 7:18; Gal 4:26 and Heb 12:22; Gal 5:4 and Heb 12:15; Gal 6:9 and Heb 10:36 [there are many more parallels between the Galatian and Roman Epistles].

'Justification by faith' may be the great exposition in Romans and the bastion defended in Galatians but is it the ground from which the Hebrews were slipping?

Central Objective of Hebrews

Hebrews is full of contrasts between the Lord and His inferiors. How does this serve the author's purpose?

If Hebrews shows the exalted place of the Saviour, does it set out in order the steps a believer might take to reach the place of holiness and security in His presence?

What inferior, earlier approaches to God does Hebrew's list (for instance 7:18,28; 8:7-8,13)?

How are the warnings and other themes connected by the author addressed?

Would you say that Hebrews is more for correction or encouragement?

How does the Holy Spirit make Hebrews such a positive book, while including the sternest of warnings?

Is it correct to say that the author of Hebrews aims to prevent failure rather than to recover the fallen or discipline them? And if so, how does he do that?

To what extent is the main thrust of the Epistle relevant to Gentile believers today?

There is a real danger of limiting the warnings of the epistle to a certain group of people or company, or to assume a warning relates to a particular danger which the Holy Spirit never intended.

How to Exhort

Who holds the primary task of exhorting believers (Heb 13:7, 17, 24) and what is your definition of this group of people?

List the writer's expressions of endearment for his readers and a similar exhortation used today.

From what does he say his concerns originate (see 13:7,16,19,22; 10:24)?

Why did the author include himself in some of the warnings?

After interpretations comes application: what does the key verse (13:22) tell us of the author's way of bringing home the meaning?

Note down the examples of the author challenging his readers to ask questions (the interrogatory method of exhortation). Which one of these is rhetorical, and which are intended to be answered by the readers?

What do you understand by the expression 'severe punishment' or 'without mercy' (10:28,29)?

What should be the place of such exhortation based on the strong warnings for today?

Should accusations accompany warnings?

How much should the Godly threat of judgement, chastisement and loss be used to exhort believers?

Exhortation to Avoid Falling

Is it clearer *from* what the readers might fall, or *into* what they could fall?

Pick out the author's statements of the believers' assurance.

What is the particular significance of the writer's conclusion in Heb 6:9?

What are the various ways the author advises his readers to avoid the dangers he sees?

Can 'rest' be equated with faith?

Look for the thread of godly optimism in the warning passages.

What connection has persecution with wavering (Hebrews chapters 12 and 13)?

What past experiences ought to bolster the believers' confidence?

What are the author's concerns about 'our profession' (Heb 3:1; 4:14; 10:23)?

Study the word 'lest' (AV) or 'so that' (NIV) in Heb 2:1; 3:12,13; 4:1,11; 11:24,28; 12:3,13.

What is the reason for the author's emphasis on 'to the end' (Heb 3:6,14; 6:11)?

Examine the 'consider' passages as a basis for the believers' meditation and stability (Heb 3:1; 7:4; 10:24; 12:3).

Some of these questions beg answers which assume a particular viewpoint on the Epistle depending on your own previous knowledge base. If that is the case then, of course, you should look for reasons to justify a different answer that is in keeping with Scripture.

Developing and forming an idea

Heb 10:19-25: In this passage the author applies a previous discussion of the high priestly work of Jesus. Here you can see the main trunk of the subject, not the High Priesthood of Jesus which is too great a subject, nor the sub-idea of boldness to enter the holy place, but instead the relevant question which asks, how is it believers can enter into the presence of God[100]? The following are possible answers:

1. Draw near to God with the assurance that comes from a cleansed heart and life.
2. Hold unswervingly to the hope you profess.
3. Spur one another on to love and good works.

Can this same application be worked through another passage in Hebrews, such as Heb 13:1-9 or 12:4-13?

We have come to the end of your time learning how to interpret the Bible using the book of Hebrews and so we finish with the first question that we asked at the end of chapter one. How has your interpretation

---

[100] Robinson H 2001 2nd ed. *Expository Preaching: Principles and Practice* IVP England

and study pattern of the Bible changed during the reading of this book and what would you say is your preferred method of studying the Bible?

No matter how often we look into Biblical truths or read the Word of God, there is always something new which reaches out and holds onto the fabric of our faith. This is the work of the Holy Spirit, sanctifying us, making us holy *'through the sacrifice of the body of Jesus Christ once for all'.*

NOTES

The Matter Before the Method

Epilogue

Glorify the Lord with me: let us exalt His name together

Psalm 34:3

To all those who have chosen to read this book there is a message from the Author:

Wallingford

2nd June 1987

Dear Friends,

We very much appreciate your kindly wishes. I find it difficult to settle down to anything which requires concentration. I can manage perhaps four hours work either at home or in Oxford, and half a mile walking at least, but I am particularly good at sleeping anywhere, any time! Tomorrow I am to try to give the first lecture of one hour (on tree roots and buildings). My progress really has been good, but I am impatient and cannot always see the changes for the better that other people notice. I am able to drive the car but singing is a problem!

The attention of the hospital service here was beyond any expectation: the number of x-rays, isotope scans, whole body scanning, biopsy with fibreglass optics before the operation was amazing. In the event they performed a rather more extensive Pneumonectomy and removed the whole of the right lung. In the meantime, they tell me to live as I would have done in any case, that is, to ignore the whole affair. I find this easy to do because my hopes are beyond this life, and I look forward to being with Christ, which, the Bible says, is far better. Before He was crucified for us the Lord Jesus himself said, 'I go to prepare a place for you.... in my Father's house.' To quote again, this is like an 'Anchor of the soul...sure and steadfast'. It takes away any worry that Joan and I might naturally feel. I think it also helps our friends who have been so supportive spiritually and practically.

My mind is remarkably clear; far clearer than after my previous serious operation in 1982. I have been able to teach my student who is preparing for examination, and I can attend to all my correspondence as well as read (intelligently I hope!) the abstracting journals plus 'Nature Forestry' and so on. The only real difficulty is to sit and attend to writing for prolonged periods. Thus, in trying to write a book for Christians on the interpretation of scripture (you encouraged me along this line you remember) the concentration makes one very weary and I find it takes a great deal of discipline to sit down and recommence. However, I would not be at all surprised that this proves to be the very primary reason for the success of the surgical operation. I have also been able to start teaching the young people in my church again and this I find rewarding.

Of course, Joan joins me in sending our best wishes with our prayers for you all. We carry such happy memories of Dehra Dun.

With sincerest greetings,
Evan and Joan Reynolds

'Hesed'
Wallingford

9th November 1987

We have hesitated to send an end of year letter of this kind partly because it seems rather impersonal (but please receive it with our sincerest greetings) and partly in case our news seems rather 'heavy'. People have been incredibly thoughtful for us, both in practical ways and in praying for us most faithfully. Whatever our Gracious God displays as His perfect will over the next weeks, we are convinced that the fellowship shown in these ways has brought Him more pleasure than physical sacrifices or incense. It is not for us to guess how He will answer this volume of prayer, but we feel sure He will glorify His own Holy Name.

It will hardly be news now to most folk, but in the first week of November, I retired from the University through ill-health. This was after 28 years of work I can only describe as most enjoyable. It was an inestimable privilege to know that it was the place the Lord had prepared. After some illness in 1982, it was clearly in the Lord's purposes that we were able to spend seven busy months in Northern India with Emmanuel and Beulah Raj; staying at their school. Amidst the research I had planned to do and the sewing of uniforms for the schoolgirls (which I didn't do!) we thoroughly enjoyed the spiritual experiences with the believers at Dehra Dun.

The gracious ways of God were evident in that within a few months of returning a recurrence of previous problems required a lung operation. More recently further development has affected the other lung and the brain. As always, we are able in part to see His purposes working out. In not being able to preach the gospel or teach the Good Word of God, I must place more emphasis on writing and look forward to being able to complete a study on the Interpretation of Scripture based on the Epistle to the Hebrews.

Epilogue

Meanwhile the support and sweet fellowship of the believers here in Wallingford are very precious indeed to us. Further visits to hospital are probably in store for us and maybe loss of faculties but having a Saviour and the Hope of His promise, we could not be 'better off.'

We join in sending our love in the Lord Jesus Christ
Evan and Joan Reynolds

23rd December 1987

A transcription of Dave Corps' diary, the last person to see Evan Reynolds in hospital:

Fairly mild today. Left (the house) 2pm. Saw Joan. Paul is down. Ruth and David come this evening. Mark and Heather come tomorrow. Stayed 35 mins and then to see Evan. Mar stayed in car. He looked quite a bit better. He was reading Colossians 1 and writing notes. These included a letter to the Assembly. Evan said he felt he wanted to write to both his friends (letter at Christmas) and the Assembly. We talked about my, and his work testimony. Evan seemed almost as concerned about his as I am about mine. He need not worry. Evan was pleased he and Joan had talked about the Hymns he wanted (for his funeral). This affected his emotions. I told him I'd just signed my new will and made my funeral arrangements. This leaves a tidy testimony behind. Told Evan I shall find his passing harder than Father's to bear. He was wanting to see my 'Family Base' mag. Must bring it over when I come in Jan. Thank you Lord for another privileged meeting with Evan. Felt compelled to stay with him. Don't know why. Had a good chat. I stayed one and a half hours. Talked re: need for more issues to be taught in Assembly fellowship. Evan was concerned for Joan having to take him for his current radiotherapy after Christmas (at present he's in hospital but as he's better they want him to be an outpatient). Talked re: Guildford job. Geoffrey Reynolds (Evan's brother) knows a believer there. Left a copy of my job description. Read part Psalm 34, prayed, left 6.30.

Dave was woken the next morning by two phone calls, one from Mr Herbert and then Pauline Cummins to say that Evan had passed on. He commented that it was a 'sad day'.

22nd March 1988
Government of India
Forest Research Institute and Cos.
New Forest,
Dehra Dun.

Dear Mrs Reynolds,

Your letter dated 25th Feb 1988 was received with great shock to all of us. We were wondering all the time why there was no news from you for such a long time in spite of repeated letters, but it never occurred to us that Dr Reynolds was no more. Even Dr Richard Hardings who visited this Institute did not disclose this news. Anyway, it was a great shock to learn the sad demise of Dr Reynolds who was so dear to all of us who worked with him although one could apprehend it from the contents of Dr Reynolds last letters. To me it is a great personal loss. A condolence meeting was held in Forest Influences Branch on 15th March 1988 to mark the death of Dr Reynolds. Silence was observed in his memory and prayer made. The copy of resolution is being sent with this letter. We pray that the departed soul may rest in peace.

With best wishes and regards,
Yours sincerely,
Dr RM Singhel

Condolence Meeting held on 15th March 1988 at the Forest Influences Branch, F.R.I. and colleges, Dehra-Dun, India on the sad demise of Dr E.R.C. Reynolds.

Resolution

This meeting of the officers and staff members of the Forest Influences Branch and Environmental Research Station, F.R.I. and Colleges, Dehra Dun place on record their profound sense of grief at the sad demise of Dr E.R.C. Reynolds, Lecturer in Forestry, University of Oxford, who left for his heavenly abode on 23rd December 1987 at Oxford. The house conveys their deep sympathy and condolences to the bereaved family and pray that the departed soul may rest in peace.

It is resolved that a copy of this resolution be conveyed to the bereaved family.

ALL SHOPS AND OFFICES WILL BE CLOSED FOR THAT DAY.

Epilogue

The End of the Rainbow

My suitcase stands in a brightened hall
and in a dream, I kiss goodbye
the things I've known and touched.
Inside are packed essential needs,
With tissues of love, labelled
'Fragile, with care.'

Everything ready? A voice far off
I pat my wallet – it is bursting
With wealth, of a lifetime spent
And memories crammed into bags with zips.

Behind that door
Is a brand new life
And my pockets are burning
With wisdom to spend.

I turn, pick up the suitcase,
Light with a heavy load.
It leaves a trail of dust
On the floor and the draught
From the door turns it into gold
-precious and scattered.
A deep breath now, shoulders squared
And the end of the Rainbow is at my feet.

Ruth Aird November 1997

ACKNOWLEDGMENTS

As Editor I have strived to keep the concept of the original manuscript and deep spiritual desire of my father intact so that the reader would benefit in the way he would have wanted. More than anything else he had a passion for passing on his Biblical knowledge to the next generation, wanting them to be able to interpret the Scriptures in the way that would best reflect their relationship with the Lord Jesus. At the same time I have endeavoured to sensitively add references from the past thirty three years reflecting the views of recent writers. I take full responsibility for the exercises which were added to each chapter and around two thirds of additional explanatory text. However, the final version of this study guide is, I hope, a blended version of the original unique and creative study guide and subsequent additions for which I owe many thanks to the following:

The Reynolds and the Aird family, including wives and husbands, have provided a backbone of encouragement and support as I bombarded them with email after email! They patiently read each manuscript, offering various comments which have gone into the mix of the whole project. Malcom Davis, a student from the early days at Oxford and now an author in his own right, allowed me to use him as a consultant all the way through the project. Bill Stevely, also a PhD student from Oxford, and David Monkcom another Oxford student, spent many precious hours reading through the text, correcting and fine tuning the manuscript to make it what it is today. I would also like to thank Alison Bowie and Eric Scott for reading the original manuscript and making suggestions which provided the foundation for planning the book. Finally, Jenny Robertson, my colleague in writing from the Scottish Fellowship of Christian Writers, made it her mission to read through the manuscript, giving me helpful and wonderfully encouraging suggestions.

Acknowledgments

Thank you all of you for enabling the publishing of a book which has been long in the writing, but will I hope, be a tribute to my father and accomplish what he wanted it to, giving glory to the One who is our Lord in heaven.

Ruth Aird

REFERENCES

Berkhof L 1950 Principles of Biblical Interpretation (sacred hermeneutics) Baker Bookhouse Grand Rapids, Michigan USA

Bowman J 1963 *Hebrews, James 1 and 2 Peter Layman's Bible Commentaries* SCM Press UK

Bullinger W *The Companion Bible* Marshall Pickering Oxford University Press

Catchpole R 2021 Dispensational Theology (1) Lamp and Light The Society for Distributing Hebrew Scriptures January/February

Catchpole R 2021 Dispensational Theology (2) Lamp and Light The Society for Distributing Hebrew Scriptures March /April

Chafer L 1974 Revised by Walvoord J Major Bible Themes Zondervan Press USA

Darby J 1961 New Translation Bible Stow Hill Bible and Tract Depot Kingston UK available at: https://www.biblegateway.com/ versions/Darby-Translation-Bible/#booklist accessed Nov 2021

Dillehay J 2020 Jesus according to the New Tetament's most quoted Psalm available at: https://www.thegospelcoalition.org/article/ psalm-110/ accessed Nov 2021

Davis F Hays R 2003 *The Art of Reading Scripture* edited by Davis and Hays Eerdmans' Publishing Com USA/UK

E-Sword 2021 Interlinear Bible Commentary from six Expositors available at: https://www.e-sword.net/ accessed November 2021

Farrar F 1912 ed The Epistle to the Hebrews Cambridge Greek Testament for school and colleges Cambridge University Press UK

References

Gooding D 1976 *An Unshakeable Kingdom Ten Studies on the Epistle to the Hebrews* Everyday Publications Canada

Guzik D 2004 *Verse by Verse Commentary Hebrews* The Enduring Word Commentary Series Enduring Word Media USA

Harmon M 2017 *Asking the Right Questions: A practical guide to understanding and applying the Bible* Crossway Publishing USA

Heading J 1979 *Types and Shadows in the Epistle to the Hebrews* Gospel Tract Publications Glasgow UK

Jamieson, Fauset and Brown 1973 Commentary on the Whole Bible Eerdmans Publications

Kelly W (undated) *Introductory Lectures: the Epistle to the Hebrews* Bible Truth Publisher Illinois Available at: http://biblecentre.org/content.php?mode=7&item=271 accessed Nov 2021

Kruger M 2021 Hebrews: An Anchor for the Soul The Good Book Company UK

Lane T Tripp P 2008 *How People Change* New Growth Press USA

Mackison N 2020 Christian Doctrine Lectures: Lecture 5 Divine Changelessness - Immutability Edinburgh Theological Seminary, October

McKeen J 2020 *The Model Sermon: Principles of Preaching from the Book of Hebrews* Published by Christianity Today

McQuoid J 2016 *Hebrews: The Daily discipline of a Devoted Life* 10 Publishing UK

Morris L 1978 Understanding the New Testament Published by Holman UK

Moule H 1977 *Studies in Hebrews* Kregel Publications USA

Murray A 1894 The Holiest of all: A Commentary on Hebrews ISBN 0-883 68-523-X

Naish R 1921 Spiritual Arithmetic Published by Thynne and Co London UK

Newberry's New English Study Bible 1970 Oxford and Cambridge University Press

Olyott S 2010 *I wish someone would explain Hebrews to Me!* Banner of Truth Edinburgh UK

Phillips J 1970 *Ring of Truth* Hodder and Stoughton

Phillips J 1984 *The Price of Success* Hodder and Stoughton

Reynolds E Davis M 1988 *Types, Patterns and Shadows* Precious Seed November/December Vol 39 No.6

Robinson H 2001 2nd ed. *Expository Preaching: Principles and Practice* IVP England

Ryrie C 1965 Dispensationalism today Moody Press

Sauer E 1955 The Arena of Faith Paternoster Press UK

Schofield 1954 *Reference Bible and Commentary* Oxford University Press

Sprent J 1892 Gleanings in the Hebrews The Witness Glasgow Scotland

Sonic Light 2021 Bible Commentary Dr Thomas Constable available at https://www.planobiblechapel.org/tcon/notes/html/nt/hebrews/hebrews.htm accessed November 2021

Stibbs A 1954 2nd Ed New Bible Commentary Inter-varsity Fellowship

Traub W 2021 'How to interpret and apply the OT today' Lecture 6 on Hebrews Edinburgh Theological Seminary

Vine WE 1997 *Expository dictionary of Old and New Testament Words* Nelsons USA

Vlach M 2022 Dispensational Theology Available at: https://www.thegospelcoalition.org/essay/dispensational-theology/ accessed January 2022

Westcott B 2nd Ed 1892 The Epistle to the Hebrews: The Greek text with notes and essays Macmillan and Co Scotland

References

Weymouth R 1909 3rd Ed the New Testament in Modern Speech James Clarke and Co London

Wright J S 1955 *Interpreting the Bible* Intervarsity Fellowship UK

Wright T 2003 *Hebrews for Everyone* Published by Society for Promoting Christian Knowledge UK

Zuck, R 1991 *Basic Bible Interpretation: A Practical Guide to Discovering Biblical Truth* Victor Publishing USA UK

Appendix 1

Explanation of the significance of numbers of times biblical characters mentioned in the book of Hebrews

The significance of biblical characters in the book of Hebrews is the mention of Moses nine times (as he was the Hebrew law giver this makes his contribution significantly important). Abraham and Melchizedek are mentioned eight times and again to the Hebrew mind they are fathers of the nation – one literally and the other spiritually. The other people mentioned are faithful witnesses.

Be careful to look at the significance of scripture and names especially if duplicated. Put them in the context of the history of the Old Testament and the number of times they are mentioned in your study as they can (but not always) influence the credence you put on them in interpretation. This knowledge of Old Testament characters can show New Testament application.

The following data table shows the characters in the book of Hebrews.

Table 4: Numerical table of characters in Hebrews

No. of Characters	11	6	2	1	0	0	0	2	1
No. of Times Mentioned	1	2	3	4	5	6	7	8	9

1 person was mentioned 9 times
2 people were mentioned 8 times
0 people were mentioned 7 times
0 people were mentioned 6 times
0 people were mentioned 5 times
1 person was mentioned 4 times
2 people were mentioned 3 times

Appendix 1

6 people were mentioned 2 times
11 people were mentioned 1 time

If we take a newspaper as an example and look at the number of times someone (a) is mentioned then it might be 20 times, someone else (b) might be 15 times (depends on what bias the newspaper has). This means a's stories are more significant than b's (again depending on your politics). As we collate all the names mentioned in the newspaper, we can create a tally of the number of people getting however many mentions. When we look at this tally, we realise that no one gets just 6 mentions. There are some with 5 mentions and some with 7, but no one gets exactly 6 mentions.

If a character has more mentions than others, then the Holy Spirit is trying to point you to look at that person more. The one who has 6 mentions is just a statistic rather than a place marker — the person with 11 mentions is someone to look at more closely.

The interesting anomaly is the book of Esther — clearly a book pointing to God's over-riding love of his people and concern for their preservation. However, as God is not mentioned at all, we might assume He is of no interest whatsoever. We know that this is not true — but look at the significance of the mentions of Esther and Mordecai and the trust they put in God and not in their own understanding. This makes meaning out of the numbers placed in the Bible at strategic points.

APPENDIX 2

Types, Patterns and Shadows: Evan Reynolds and Malcolm Davis
Precious Seed November/December 1988 Vol 39 no. 6

A most important ability cultivated by the Holy Spirit in a Christian is the interpretation of the Old Testament pictures to shed light on New Testament doctrine. The tool for the task is 'Biblical Typology'. It rests on three divine and important principles. Firstly, God is immutable and consistent in the way He deals with His creatures throughout history. Secondly, God is in sovereign control of historical events from first to last. Finally, He reveals Himself progressively throughout the ages of human history. These principles operate from Genesis to Revelation, so that scripture is not merely historical, but is interpretable to lead the believer to a fuller knowledge of His Lord and Saviour.

We have an infallible guide to the use of typology in the way that New Testament writers employed some of the Old Testament pictures. They gave the illustrations several somewhat distinct technical names (which we shall try to understand), and so distinguished them from the New Testament pictures to which they gave other names.

Here is a table to show, at a glance, the five important and interrelated Greek words, and in italics, the English words which the translators used in the Authorised Version in just four chapters of the epistle to the Hebrews. It was the translators' deliberate policy to introduce this variety, but it can make the student's task harder. To make matters worse, in different contexts there are other Greek words translated by these English words, and other English renderings of these five Greek words. If we look in turn at the way the Holy Spirit guided the New Testament writers to use these Greek words when interpreting the Old Testament, we shall be blessed in our Bible study. We have to admit that the two words 'type' and 'antitype' so commonly used in ministry today, although these are obviously the first two Greek words in our table, do not appear in our Authorised Version (but see the marginal translation of TUPOS in 1 Cor 10:11).

Appendix 2

Table 5: Greek/English words used by translators in the Authorised Version

TUPOS	ANTITUPOS	HUPODEIGMA	SKIA	PARABOLE
(pattern)	(figure)	(pattern)	(shadow)	(figure)
Hebrews 8:5	Hebrews 9:24	Hebrews 9:23	Hebrews 8:5	Hebrews 9:9
		(example) Hebrews 8:5	Hebrews 10:1	Hebrews 11:19

TUPOS is the most inconsistently translated. Coming from a root indicating the impression made by a blow, the word seems to have the senses, 'one of the class', of the same genre', 'one to which the rest should aspire', or even 'corresponding to'.

In Rom 5:14 Adam in humanity, not in his transgression and condemnation, was the 'type' (AV 'figure') to which class the Lord belonged by His gracious stoop (compare 1 Cor 15:45 and Heb 2:6-9).

The cloud, the Red Sea, the manna, and the water from the rock united the Israelites to God's man, but this did not prevent them from being judged for their sin (1 Cor 10:6, 11: AV 'examples' and 'ensamples' respectively). This is a class with which we do not want to be associated: a comparison we should avoid. Judgement 'happened to them typically' (JND footnote).

Stephen on trial told of the construction of the tabernacle (Acts 7:44) and emphasised Moses' obedience to God's will in making it 'according to the fashion that he had seen'. When Ex 25:40 is quoted again in Heb 8:5 the AV translators gave 'pattern' for TUPOS. To render it 'model' in some translations is clearly wrong as models are copied from patterns.

Thus, we see that TUPOS stresses similarity. An illustration might be the typewriter. The letters on the paper correspond to the metal type which hits the ribbon. So, we delight to learn from similarities to Old Testament pictures or are warned of resemblances. Note that it is not the same as 'archetype' which emphasises the priority, if not superiority, of the pattern. 'Type' may be applied to the pattern or the copy, the original or the impression.

ANTITUPOS, although it certainly does not convey the reality which the type or symbol represents (the meaning of the English 'antitype'), it does draw a contrast to a degree which TUPOS does not: the prefix suggests that it is 'against' or 'in place of'. The correspondence is a mould to a cast. This is rather lost by the AV figure.

The holy places which Levitical priests entered were distinctly ANTITUPA of the Holy Places in Heaven to which the Superior Christ has right of access to take His place in Divine audience (Heb 9:24).

Explanations of the use of ANTITUPOS in 1 Pet 3:21 (AV 'figure') are contradictory. The word 'also' suggests that both flood water and baptismal water are types (one from the Old Testament and the other from the New) of salvation through Jesus Christ's resurrection which procures the witness before God of cleared consciences (see too Vine's Dictionary Vol 2). This may help us to appreciate that even a New Testament symbol is of no value unless it draws our attention to the Saviour's centrality.

HUPODEIGMA derives from the word meaning 'to show'. That is, it indicates something held up for consideration either to follow, to teach or to warn. It generally refers to the most obvious lesson to draw from the Old Testament example. The most touching use is when the Lord washed the disciples' feet and said, 'I left you an example' (John 13:15). Only once does the word appear without its prefix, HUPO-. This prefix perhaps suggests that the examples need discernment: that they are for disciples who want to discover the secrets of a sanctified life.

'Pattern' cannot be the correct translation of the word in Heb 9:23, as the heavenly counterparts of the tabernacle and its vessels have been designated the 'pattern' in Heb 8:5. Better suggestions have been 'similitudes', 'copies' or 'representations'. The translators' difficulty was that Heb 9:23 refers to things, not a person, so that 'example' would not do. Even in Heb 8:5 HUPODEIGMA is more correctly applied not to the priests, but to the economy they served. Thus, it is referring to the 'visualized' tabernacle model of the invisible heavenly things, a tangible teaching aid to conceive the heavenly things. The tabernacle is definitely not to be copied: it is a 'copy' or 'sketch' itself. Any misinterpretation is corrected by the addition of the complementary idea of its being a 'shadow'.

SKIA is the word for this 'shadow' in complete contrast to 'the very image' (Col 2:17), 'substance' or 'the body' itself (Heb 10:5). We often think today of the 'shadow cabinet', 'shadow pricing' and so on. A shadow only exists by reason of the light shining on a real object. Where there is a shadow, there must be a reality close by. The shadow is an insubstantial, flat, unlighted area. Thus, in scripture this word is used to differentiate between things which are being compared. One of the pair is in the shade of the other, either because it is for a time obscured, or because the Holy Spirit is emphasising that it is less important.

Thus, if we look again at Heb 8:5 the word HUPODEIGMA reminds us that the tabernacle system is a representation or example. But lest we think it is to be awarded equal importance to the spiritual counterparts which exist today, it is in the same breath, SKIA. The tabernacle was real enough for the Levitical priests to serve, but it is put into second place as a shadow of that eternal place where Jesus ministers. But being a shadow, the tabernacle makes us look up for the reality so that a study of that system will be a blessing to a believer.

Heb 10:1 uses 'shadow' in the sense of 'foreshadow'. The emphasis is not so much that the law is insubstantial itself, but rather that it casts an insubstantial shadow of future things. The law is not an exact replica of the coming 'good things' in a general sense, (but Christ and salvation in particular Heb 9:16-18) and is therefore ineffective in satisfying seekers.

Similarly, in Col 2:17 Paul writes of some observances of the ceremonial law as a shadow cast forward through the ages, across the dispensations. The substantial body of which these rites are only shadows is the Person of Christ (John 5:39; Luke 24:27).

In sum, attention is diverted from the shadow. The Old Testament shadows are superseded, but there is a perpetual danger of shadows becoming snares for those who have escaped from these rudiments (Col 2:20). After the revelation of the New Testament, the shadows are no longer to be the means of approaching God: their time of usefulness has passed, and they are worse than useless if trust is placed in them. In every way 'Christ is the end of the law' (Rom 10:4). SKIA is the least positive way of interpreting the Old Testament.

PARABOLE, as might be guessed, is hardly ever translated into English by any other word than 'parable'. However, twice it is applied to the interpretation of the OT and translated 'figure'. Essentially it is used when two ideas are deliberately brought together so that the comprehensible may illuminate the less tangible, or more abstract, thought. Usually, the comparison is extended to several facets. It is unusual for contrast to be intended, though it could occur. The fact that the word used for the NT parables is also made to refer to the OT pictures strikingly suggests that the method the Lord demonstrated with worked examples to interpret His parables (Mt 13:10-23, 36-43) is similar to the way we should understand OT stories (as in Heb 11:19) or the deliberately constructed illustration, the tabernacle (Heb 9:9). In the latter case, the Newberry[101] margin actually has 'parables.'

The Holy Spirit originated the significance of the tabernacle construction (Heb 9:8) to help believers in the Gospel age (R.V. 'A parable for the time now present': the AV gives a wrong idea in having 'then present', and even JND's complicated footnote unnaturally restricts the parable to an interim age). The gifts, offerings, sanctuary, and high priest (Heb 9:11,12) must all be interpreted in terms of the New Covenant. The tabernacle model itself (or the substituted temple) would not long be allowed to coexist with the new dispensation ('the way into the holiest was not yet made manifest while as the first tabernacle was yet standing'). There came a point when the model had to be laid aside since its servitors were in conflict with the gospel. Whereas the description in the Old Testament is a blessed illustration for us, it must not be physically projected into the church age as clergy, ritual, and sanctuary.

Heb 11:19 tells of the figurative resurrection of Isaac. The words 'in a figure' undoubtedly refer to this specific point in the story, although

---

[101] Newberry's New English Study Bible 1970 Oxford and Cambridge University Press

just as certainly the whole story is figurative, making us look at the counterpart, our blessed Lord's journey to the land of Moriah to offer Himself.

In conclusion, what general lesson may we draw from our studies of the words used to describe the great Old Testament illustrations of New Testament doctrine? We do not find that some of the illustrations are types, that others are shadows, and yet another is an example. Rather the words are used to complement one another. This is obvious in Heb 8:5 where 'shadow' (SKIA) and 'example' (HUPODEIGMA) are used together to speak of the tabernacle system. But in Heb 9:23-24 'example' (HUPODEIGMA) and 'figures' (ANTITUPON) are used of virtually the same illustration, which is called a 'figure' (PARABOLE) in Heb 9:9. Then all these relate back to the glorious 'pattern', 'fashion' or 'type' (TUPOS) of Heb 8:5 and Acts 7:44. So we must endeavour to bear in mind the meanings of all five of these Greek words when studying any Old Testament types, in order more fully to appreciate the Great Antitype, the Lord Jesus Christ, and His heavenly purposes.

SUBJECT INDEX

Aaron 125, 134, 157, 164-166

Abel 103, 130, 131

Abraham 26, 69, 84, 99, 109, 129, 130, 154, 164, 206

Ahab 176, 179-181

Allegory 65, 68, 139, 144, 145, 149

Allusions 74, 75, 103, 113, 123, 135

Anthropological 49

Antitype 140, 142, 165-167, 208, 210, 213

Antonyms 92

Apocrypha 75

Aramaic 87, 88, 94, 135

Baptism 23, 142

Biographical 32, 44-46, 51, 131, 154, 167

Ceremonial 112, 116, 134, 151, 211

Chronological 32, 44-46, 102, 103

Colours 144

Comparative 45, 89, 96, 114

Concordance 32, 47, 60, 96, 124

Context 30, 39, 44, 48, 49, 52, 58, 76, 77, 79, 88, 92, 99, 102, 123, 124, 138, 156, 165, 206

Covenant 17, 45, 69, 84, 90, 95, 108, 109, 113-115, 125, 126, 134, 135, 170-173, 185, 212

Cultural 49, 76, 97, 126, 135, 136, 152

Dictionaries 35, 48, 49, 82, 94

Digital 17, 18, 49

Dispensations 107, 108, 110-113, 115, 159, 211

Equip 30, 35

Etymology 92

Exegesis 30, 37, 75

Exposition 6, 15, 30, 39, 46, 58, 86, 88, 107, 120, 127, 172, 187

Ezekiel 144, 172

Figurative 97, 98, 120, 212

Geographical 44, 49, 76, 97, 145, 156, 176

Greek 30, 37, 38, 47, 51, 53, 83, 84, 86-89, 92, 94-97, 118, 139, 140, 142, 155, 158, 159, 171-173, 202, 204, 208, 209, 213

Hermeneutics 30, 38, 202

High Priest 20, 78, 125, 126, 164-166, 168, 173, 212

Historical 31, 38, 43, 56, 76, 102, 139, 140, 165, 166, 208

Holiness 56, 65, 112, 126, 151, 176, 179-182, 187

Holy Spirit 9, 21, 24, 30-32, 36, 38, 39, 44, 46, 48, 50-52, 56, 57, 62, 63, 65, 67, 69, 74, 75, 78, 81, 83, 85, 89, 102-104, 110, 112, 118, 124, 130, 134, 140, 141, 155, 164, 170-172, 176, 177, 187, 190, 207, 208, 211, 212

Illustration 20, 39, 99, 133, 142, 149, 172, 209, 212, 213

Immutability 69, 70, 113, 126, 203

Interlinear 47, 94, 202

Interrogatory 45, 159, 188

Irenaeus 138

Jehoshaphat 76, 176-182

Jeremiah 125, 143, 144, 170, 172-174

Jerusalem 35, 99, 104, 152, 179, 180

Joshua 21, 77, 103, 156, 158, 159

Keywords 32, 96

Lectio Divina 71

Lexicon 53, 89, 94

Literalistic 45

Melchizedek 37, 51, 95, 99, 126, 129, 130, 139, 146, 163-168, 206

Messianic 45, 118, 163, 165

Metaphor 68, 98, 99

Moses 21, 40, 77, 96, 104, 119, 125, 126, 129, 130, 133, 141, 157-159, 165, 170, 173, 206, 209

Narrative 24, 38, 56, 104, 140, 154, 157, 160, 164, 176, 180

Noah 108, 129, 130

Numbers 17, 50, 64, 74, 89, 135, 144, 155, 157, 160, 186, 206, 207

Parables 25, 74, 87, 141, 149, 212

Paul 10, 18, 23, 67, 69, 78, 84, 93, 103, 177, 178, 185, 196, 211

Paraphrase 45, 48, 87, 88, 90, 163, 170

Peter 37, 95, 118, 144, 202

Philo 51

Priest 20, 32, 37, 77, 78, 95, 99, 125, 126, 164-166, 168, 173, 212

Promised Land 21, 40, 155, 157, 158

Prophetic 31, 36, 45, 104, 118-120

Quotations 39, 48, 67, 74-79, 83, 84, 163, 170

Redeemer 84

Rest 33, 41, 70, 77, 93, 94, 100, 103, 104, 120, 121, 126, 127, 155-161, 167, 188, 197, 198, 209

Ritual 39, 56, 114, 115, 133, 140, 143, 148, 151, 212

Sanctification 65, 66, 140, 151, 173, 176-180, 182

Saviour 59, 69, 70, 82, 95, 112, 130, 149, 151, 159, 164, 173, 187, 195, 208

Septuagint 84, 85, 94, 155

Shadow 70, 84, 139-142, 146, 149, 209, 211, 213

Sinai 69, 111, 119, 152, 159

Sword 21, 38, 63-66, 68, 89, 100, 171, 202

Synonyms 92

Tabernacle 23, 113, 126, 133-136, 141, 142, 148, 149, 151, 152, 156, 165, 167, 172, 173, 209-213

Temple 35, 148, 150, 152, 155, 166, 212

Timothy 17, 18, 29, 89, 105, 129, 176

Topical 32, 39, 45, 46, 58, 123, 125

Transform 26

Translation 47-49, 53, 82-88, 90, 94, 130, 140, 141, 155, 170, 202, 208, 210

Translators 48, 81-83, 88, 90, 97, 208-210

Typology 39, 45, 138, 139, 142, 145, 165, 170, 172, 208

Types 32, 74, 111, 139-143, 145, 146, 148, 166, 173, 203, 204, 208, 210, 213

Uzziah 166, 173

Word Study 32, 94, 155, 156, 160, 176

Worldview 120, 126

Worship 32, 64, 112, 115, 116, 134, 148, 150, 151, 159, 165, 166, 168, 176, 178

Zwingli 76